THE Social Life Cookbook

CONTENTS

INTRODUCTION

Welcome to the social life.

Whether you've got kids of your own or you are living the single life, entertaining your friends and family can be one of life's greatest pleasures – and biggest stresses! There is so much to consider – time, budget, menu planning, presentation and even the food intolerances of your guests. This book is jam-packed with solutions that will help you plan the perfect event.

We've added some great information pages in the book, alongside the recipes, to help equip you with the skills you need to take your cooking to the next level and impress your guests.

Most of the recipes in this book tend towards the indulgent, or special, as befits time spent enjoying food with friends and family. Brunch is no exception. In this section of the book you'll find a recipe for banana bread that's far removed from the everyday version – dripping in mascarpone coffee cream, fresh berries and syrup, this is a pure joy to share. Individual creme brulees for brunch are decadence in a bowl, but what a lovely idea for a sweet finish to a long brunch with friends. Savourywise, consider a deviation from the norm, like shakshuka or kedgeree. Families might enjoy a stack of crepes or pancakes for breakfast or perhaps perfectly poached eggs served with something special.

After brunch comes lunch, and when you are living the social life, long, lazy afternoons can be a highlight of time spent enjoying each other's company. Summer afternoons are an awesome opportunity to fire up the barbecue and many of the recipes in this section of the book provide great ideas for how to create perfectly charred, grilled, marinated and mouthwatering fish, meat, vegetables and even cheese on the barbecue. Pair it with some fresh and cool mocktails and you have all the ingredients for a sweet afternoon with friends or family.

In the next section of this book, we take the 'bring a plate' idea to the next level. If you are stuck for inspiration, look no further than the ideas in this section. We cover the classics here – garlic bread (with a twist) and arancini balls, but then we step it up a notch. Want to try your hand at empanada? It's not as hard as you might think. Or how about cabbage rolls? A great vegetarian option. For the sweet tooth, we have the classic Portuguese custard tart, chocolate truffles or for a bit of a flourish try the chocolate salami. In Bring a Plate we've also included lots of ideas for presentation, which you can apply to other recipes in the book too. Fun ideas such as presenting mini muffins in decorated egg cartons or creating your own labels indicating the ingredients you've used (cute and a nice heads-up for the food intolerant). These little touches take time and effort, but are worthwhile and fun to do. It's all part of the social way of living.

There should always be time in life for a good dinner party. They are a pleasure to host and to participate in. In this section, we present you with plenty of menu ideas to suit the occasion you have in mind. We have taken simple recipe ideas, such as fish and chips (gourmet-style of course) or pulled pork, and paired them with fresh and flavoursome sides that give your dinner party a

Social

[so·cial] **adjective**

marked by or passed in pleasant
companionship with friends or
associates <an active social life>

—— MERRIAM-WEBSTER

cool, contemporary edge. Desserts in this section straddle the traditional –
who can go past a good tiramisu – and the contemporary too.

In the next section, the fun really starts: it's cocktail party time. We've
presented lots of great ideas to help you plan and execute the perfect party,
from planning the food and drink menu to creating the right environment and
vibe in your venue to ensure your guests have the best time. Drinkswise, we've
got you covered for the classics (Cuba libre or Campari cocktail anyone?) and
a twist on the classic (pass the raspberry margarita!). And on the food front,
you'll find ideas in here from substantial booze-soaking snacks like potato
croquettes and bruschetta, to the more delicate rose water madaleines and
salmon canapes.

We finish the book off on a warm and cosy note, with a selection of gorgeous
recipes to help you plan for a winter's night entertaining. There are roasted
vegetables and soups, hearty lamb shanks, buttery mash and roast duck,
topped off with mini chocolate lava cakes or mulberry-mulled pears and
chocolate mousse. The recipes in this section are sure to provide you with
everything you need to ensure a fun-filled night with friends.

However you like to live your social life, and whoever you live it with, you'll
find inspiration, ideas and recipes in here to make planning and enjoying
your time together that much easier. You'll be kicking back with an espresso
martini and before you know it.

Enjoy *The Social Life!*

Brunch

FANCY FRUIT: STRAWBERRIES, RASPBERRIES, CRANBERRIES

RED BERRIES

There's something about red berries. Syrupy sweet or spine-tinglingly sour, these little red morsels are a great way to start the day. As you savour the soft succulent fruit oozing its ruby-red juices, remember this: red berries like strawberries, raspberries and cranberries might be saving your life!

What makes berries red? The red colour comes thanks to anthocyanins, which are thought to help fight disease. You never know, eating a lot of brightly coloured fruit may helping your body ward off nasties. Either way, red berries look good and taste good.

TIPS FOR FRESHNESS AND FREEZING

A tip for freezing delicate fruit such as raspberries and cranberries is to lay them out on a baking sheet in a single layer and pop in the freezer for around 4 hours. When frozen, you can decant them into a bag or tub, stick on a label and return to the freezer for up to 12 months.

An unripe punnet of strawberries can be resuscitated by cutting the strawberries in half and drizzling with balsamic vinegar and a bit of sugar – try it! The best idea is to eat fruit quickly, the same day if possible, but if not then store covered in a cool dark place for 24 hours and if you still haven't eaten them invite some friends over!

HOW TO IMPRESS YOUR FRIENDS

The best way to impress your friends over brunch? Just waft over the deck to your strawberry patch (or strawberry plants in pots if you live in a smaller space) and grab a few more fresh strawberries to top up those pancakes. Failing that, you could impress them with your trivia knowledge, such as:

Rasberries are an aggregate fruit, meaning each fruit has multiple ovaries producing drupelets around a core. Each of these is truly a fruit on its own, so each raspberry is hundreds of mini-fruit.

In days gone by, raspberries were used to clean the teeth, and as a cure for sore eyes.

Cranberries, one of the few fruits native to North America, do not grow in water. They are grown on sandy bogs or marshes. Americans consume some 180 million kg (400 million lb) of cranberries a year, 20% of that during Thanksgiving week.

Strawberries are members of the rose family. They are the only fruit to wear their seeds on the outside.

If all that fails, do this: create a home-made strawberry jelly by mixing fresh strawberry juice and prosecco with gelatine leaves. Serve!

Banana Bread with Mascarpone Coffee Cream and Pistachios

BANANA BREAD WITH A DIFFERENCE — POSHED UP AND NOSHED UP WITH SUMPTIOUS CREAM AND BERRIES

SERVES 6

BANANA BREAD

2 cups (250g, 8oz) self-raising flour

1/3 cup (50g, 2oz) brown sugar

1 tsp bicarbonate of soda

2 large ripe bananas

2 eggs, whisked

1 tsp vanilla

1 cup (250ml, 8fl oz) milk

1 cup (125g, 4oz) pecans, coarsely chopped

MASCARPONE COFFEE CREAM

250g (9oz) mascarpone cheese

4 tbsps espresso coffee, cooled

3 tbsps sifted icing sugar

BERRY SAUCE

2 cups (200g, 7 oz) frozen berries

2 tbsps sugar

½ tsp lemon juice

GARNISH

Chopped pistachio nuts, to decorate

First make the banana bread.

Preheat oven to 180°C (350°F, Gas Mark 4). Line base and sides of a loaf tin with a 20cm (8in) base in greaseproof paper.

Sift the flour into a large mixing bowl. Add sugar and bicarb, and stir thoroughly to combine.

In a medium bowl, mash bananas with a fork.

Add eggs, vanilla, milk, banana and pecans to the flour mixture and gently fold until well combined. Spoon mixture into the lined tin.

Place in the oven and bake for 45 minutes or until a skewer inserted into the centre comes out clean. Set aside to cool completely.

Next make the mascarpone cream. In a small bowl, gently mix together the mascarpone, espresso and icing sugar. Cover and place in the fridge until ready to serve.

Around 20 minutes before serving, make the berry sauce. Place the berries into a medium saucepan over a medium-high heat. Add the sugar and lemon juice and bring to a gentle boil. Reduce the heat and allow to simmer for 10 minutes uncovered until the berries are soft. Check occasionally that the sauce has not reduced too much and if it has, add a splash of water.

To assemble, cut banana bread into thick slices. Create a sandwich with two pieces, layering mascarpone cream and berry sauce on each piece, finishing with a generous serve of berry sauce. Sprinkle chopped pistachios on top to garnish.

Strawberry Parfait with Yoghurt and Granola

GET FRESH AND IMPRESS WITH THIS SWEET AND CREAMY
BREAKFAST PARFAIT

SERVES 4

COULIS

2 cups (400g, 14oz)
strawberries

¾ cup (165g, 6oz) sugar

1 tsp cinnamon

1 tsp lemon peel

2 tbsps lemon juice

PARFAIT

4 cups (800g, 1¾ lb)
strawberries

2 cups (180g, 6oz)
granola

2 cups (450g, 1lb) plain
yoghurt

4 tsps pistachio nuts,
chopped

Mint leaves, to garnish

Place 2 cups of strawberries, sugar, cinnamon, lemon peel and juice into a small saucepan and cook over a medium heat for 10 minutes, or until strawberries are soft.

Transfer to a blender and puree on medium speed until smooth.

Prepare the strawberries for the parfait by washing, hulling and slicing lengthwise.

Layer granola, strawberries, yoghurt and sauce in chilled glasses or jars. Garnish with sliced strawberries, pistachios and mint.

Mini Creme Brulee

TAKE A CLASSIC DESSERT, ADD RASPBERRIES AND CALL IT BRUNCH. YOUR FRIENDS WILL LOVE YOU FOR IT

SERVES 6

6 egg yolks

4 tbsps caster sugar

1 vanilla pod

2 cups (500ml, 1pt) cream

Extra caster sugar, to caramelise

2 cups (450g, 1lb) raspberries, to garnish

Mint leaves, to garnish

Preheat oven to 140°C (285°F, Gas Mark 1).

Place the egg yolks and sugar in a large bowl and whisk for 2-3 minutes until well combined.

Halve the vanilla pod lengthways, scrape th e seeds out and combine with the cream in a small pot. Stir the mixture. Place on the stove and bring to a boil.

Pour the cream into the egg yolk, stirring continuously. Set aside for 15 minutes until the bubbles settle.

Strain the mixture into six small ramekins. Place the ramekins into a deep baking tray. Carefully pour boiling water into the baking tray so that it comes half way up the ramekins.

Place the tray in the middle of oven and bake for 30 minutes, until the custards tremble in the centre when the tray is gently shaken.

Allow the custards to cool then cover with plastic wrap and refrigerate for 3 hours.

Remove from the fridge and sprinkle caster sugar evenly across the top of each custard. Use a kitchen blowtorch to caramelise the sugar evenly. Allow to cool for 1 minute then repeat. Place in the fridge to chill for 5 minutes, then garnish with raspberries and mint before serving.

Home-Made Plum Jam

MAKES 4 CUPS

1kg (2lb) stoned plums

½ cup (125ml, 4fl oz) water

500g (1lb, 2oz) sugar

2 tbsps lemon juice

½ vanilla pod, split lengthways

Place the plums and water into a large saucepan over medium-high heat, bring to the boil then reduce heat slightly and simmer for 20 minutes.

Add the sugar and lemon juice and stir.

Scrape the vanilla seeds from the pod and stir them in, along with the pod. Bring to the boil and then reduce the heat to a simmer until the jam has set.

Remove the vanilla pod using tongs and place the jam in an airtight container to refrigerate.

Strawberry French Toast

SERVES 3

⅔ cup (160ml, 5fl oz) milk

3 eggs, lightly whisked

¼ cup (55g, 2oz) caster sugar

Pinch of mixed spice

60g (2oz) butter

6 slices thick white bread

TO SERVE

60g (2oz) butter

½ cup (180g, 6oz) maple syrup

250g (9oz) fresh strawberries

In a bowl, combine milk, egg, sugar and mixed spice.

Heat a frying pan over a high heat and melt butter until foaming.

Dip one slice of bread at a time into the egg and milk mixture, until soaked through.

Fry bread slice for 3 minutes on each side until golden brown. Repeat with remaining bread and egg mixture.

Serve hot with butter, maple syrup and fresh berries.

Crepes Suzette

A TANGY PANCAKE WITH A CHEEKY TWIST. PILE THEM UP
FOR EVERYONE TO ENJOY

SERVES 6

ORANGE SAUCE

225g (8oz, ½ lb)
unsalted butter,
softened

2 oranges, zested

⅔ cup (160ml, 5fl oz)
orange juice

½ cup (110g, 4oz)
caster sugar

¼ cup (60ml, 2fl oz)
Grand Marnier

CREPES

60g (2oz) butter

300g (10oz) plain flour

Pinch of salt

2½ cups (625ml, 20fl
oz) milk

First make the sauce. Place the butter and orange zest in a frying pan and cook over medium heat.

Add the orange juice and whisk in the sugar until it dissolves and the sauce is bubbling. Stir in the Grand Marnier and simmer for 1 minute. Reduce heat to very low and keep warm while you make the crepes.

Melt the butter in a shallow frying pan.

Sift the flour into a bowl, then add salt, and whisk in the milk and egg. When ready to cook, whisk in the melted butter.

Heat a flat-based frying pan (or crepe pan if you have one) and pour 3 tablespoons of batter into the pan then quickly hold it up and swirl so the batter forms a thin pancake over the base of the pan. Cook for 1 minute then flip and cook for 30 seconds on the other side. Remove from the pan and set aside on baking paper. Continue to make crepes in this way until the batter has been used up.

Dip each crepe into the orange sauce using tongs, covering the whole crepe in sauce. Fold them into quarters before placing on a warm plate or platter.

Remove the zest from the sauce using tongs and set aside. Pour any remaining sauce over the crepes then spread the zest over the top in a neat line. Serve immediately.

Buckwheat Berry Pancakes

HEALTHY, WHOLESOME AND NOURISHING, THESE GLUTEN-FREE PANCAKES MAKE FOR A PERFECT START TO THE WEEKEND

SERVES 2

1 cup (125g, 4oz) buckwheat flour

1 tbsp sugar

1 tsp baking powder

1 tsp bicarbonate of soda

¼ tsp salt

1¼ cups (310ml, 10fl oz) buttermilk

1 large egg

½ tsp pure vanilla extract

Butter, to fry

Maple syrup, to serve

Berries of choice, to serve

In a medium-sized mixing bowl, mix together the flour, sugar, baking powder, bicarb and salt.

Place the buttermilk in a separate bowl and then add the egg and vanilla extract.

Pour the wet ingredients into the dry ingredients and mix until just combined – don't over mix. It's okay to have a few lumps left in the batter.

Preheat the oven to 100°C (210°F, Gas Mark ¼), and line an oven tray with baking paper.

Place a medium frying pan over a medium heat and allow it to get hot before adding a knob of butter. Pour around a quarter of a cup of batter into the frying pan. Allow the batter to spread and then cook for 2-3 minutes until bubbles start to pop up on the surface and the batter starts to look less shiny. At this point, flip the pancake over and cook on the other side for 1-2 minutes until golden.

Transfer the cooked pancake to the prepared baking tray and then place in the oven, covered with foil, to keep warm.

Repeat this process until all the batter has been used up.

Serve with berries and maple syrup.

Cornflake French Toast Sticks

A CRUNCHY TAKE ON A BREAKFAST STAPLE, THESE CUTE TOAST STICKS ARE GREAT FOR SHARING

SERVES 4

2 eggs

2 tbsps milk

½ tsp vanilla extract

¼ tsp cinnamon

2 cups (60g, 1oz) crushed cornflakes

4 slices bread, cut into thick strips

2 tbsps butter

Maple syrup and blueberries, to serve

Place the eggs, milk, vanilla and cinnamon in a large bowl and whisk till combined.

Lay the crushed cornflakes onto a clean and dry work surface, or use a plate if you prefer.

Dip each bread strip into the egg mixture and then roll it through the crushed cornflakes.

Melt the butter in a large frying pan over a medium heat.

Add crumbed bread strips a few at a time according to the size of your pan and cook for 2-3 minutes on each side until nice and crunchy.

Serve with maple syrup in a dipping bowl and blueberries to garnish.

POACHED EGGS — STRAIGHT UP AND SPRUCED UP

PERFECT POACHING

How come when you go out for breakfast your poached eggs are perfect but try it at home and it's all wobbly bits and hard bits in the wrong spot? Take heart, there are just a few simple rules to follow and you'll soon be poaching your eggs to perfection.

Pick the freshest egg you can find. That's step 1.

Step 2, bring a large non-stick frying pan (use one that has a lid) to the boil with water filled up to the half way mark. Just water, no salt (will make the egg go wispy), no vinegar (not necessary).

Step 3: turn the heat right down, to around a 2 on your hotplate. Never try to poach an egg in boiling water – it will break apart. Gently crack the egg into the water. If you find it easier, crack the egg into a small bowl first and then gently pour into the water. Repeat with up to 4 eggs at a time depending on the size of your pan. Experiment with this, you might prefer to cook only 2 at a time. Put a lid on the pan.

Step 4: Set a timer for 3½ minutes for a runny yolk, and 4 minutes for a harder yolk. Walk away, chat to your friends, or pour some more coffee.

Step 5: When the timer dings, remove the eggs with a slotted spoon and place on a piece of paper towel to drain. Then slide the egg onto a plate or toast, and serve.

SPRUCE IT UP

Perfect poached eggs are pretty good on toast just as they are. But with so many options for sprucing them up it would be remiss not to try. Instead of the traditional variety, try avocado hollandaise. To make this dairy-free alternative, simply blend avocado with lemon juice and warm water. Or try a yoghurt-based hollandaise, a fresh alternative which is great served with green veggies such as asparagus or spinach. For something smoky, why not try a Mexican flavour, such as a honey chipotle lime sauce?

Rye? Wholemeal? Sourdough? Poached eggs on toast is the gold standard, but to mix things up a bit why not consider serving your eggs on tortillas, waffles, muffins, polenta cakes or hash browns? Or, forget about toast altogether and serve your poached eggs with a lovely salad or ratatouille, or in a bowl with Asian greens and fried tofu, or on top of kedgeree, with wilted greens or roasted vegetables. Don't forget about fresh herbs. Mix and match according to your other ingredients. Coriander or dill are good with seafood, parsley works well with tomato-based sauces, and sage is the perfect accompaniment where mushrooms are the hero. So many options to enjoy!

Hazelnut Dukkah

SERVES 2

DUKKAH

½ cup (80g, 3oz) sesame seeds

2 tbsps coriander seeds

2 tbsps cumin seeds

1 cup (125g, 4oz) hazelnuts

1 tsp flaked sea salt

2 tsps freshly ground black pepper

Dry roast the sesame, coriander and cumin seeds in a frying pan until aromatic and slightly golden. Add hazelnuts and roast until golden and aromatic.

Using a mortar and pestle, or a grinder, grind the ingredients for the dukkah together to a coarse powder.

Hollandaise Sauce

SERVES 2

2 egg yolks

2 tsps water

2 tsps lemon juice

5 tbsps butter

Pinch of salt and pepper

½ tsp fresh dill, chopped

In a small heatproof bowl, beat the egg yolks then combine with water and lemon juice.

Bring a medium-sized saucepan of water to a rapid boil and then reduce the heat to low. Place the heatproof bowl into the saucepan and stir very gently ensuring that the eggs do not scramble.

Gradually add the butter 1 tablespoon at a time, whisking vigorously. Add the salt, pepper and dill and continue to whisk until the sauce has thickened. If too thick, add a dash of warm water or additional lemon juice. When sauce has reached desired consistency, remove from the heat.

This recipe makes enough sauce to generously cover four poached eggs.

SMOKED SALMON

Once prohibitively expensive, smoked salmon is now a common and relatively affordable item on the supermarket shelf. It's hard to know what you are buying without trying, but look out for a soft-orange colour, not too pink nor too dark. Also keep an eye out for special flavoured varieties, which can add a nice touch to your meal.

Kedgeree

TREAT YOUR MATES TO A BIG BOWL OF THIS ANGLO-INDIAN DELIGHT FOR BREAKFAST

SERVES 12

400g (14oz) smoked cod fillets

1¼ cups (300ml, 10fl oz) milk

2 tbsps butter

1 small onion, finely chopped

1 tsp mild curry powder

1½ cups (235g, 7oz) basmati rice

1¼ cups (300ml, 10fl oz) vegetable stock

4 eggs

½ lemon, zested

Small handful parsley, finely chopped

Place the fish and milk in a large frying pan over a medium-high heat and bring to a gentle simmer. Cook uncovered for 3-4 minutes or until the fish starts to flake. Remove from the heat and strain, reserving the poaching liquid. Wipe the frying pan clean with paper towel.

Using the same frying pan, heat the butter on a medium-high heat until just melted. Add the onion and cook for 5-6 minutes or until softened. Next, stir in the curry powder and rice and stir well until all the grains are coated.

Add the reserved poaching liquid and vegetable stock to the pan. Reduce the heat to medium-low. Stir a couple of times to combine the ingredients and then leave alone to cook for 12 minutes. When cooked the rice should be tender and all the liquid absorbed.

Meanwhile place the eggs in a medium-sized saucepan of cold water. Bring to a rapid boil for 2½ minutes. Remove from the pan, rinse with cold water and set aside to cool. Peel the eggs and cut into quarters.

Place the rice in a large bowl and fluff up with a fork. Then add the flaked cooked smoked cod, lemon zest and parsley, stirring through carefully. Spoon onto serving plates and top with the quartered eggs.

Shakshuka

WANT EGGS BUT BORED OF POACHED AND SCRAMBLED?
LOOK NO FURTHER THAN THIS FILLLING AND FLAVOURSOME OPTION

SERVES 4

3 cups (600g, 21oz) cherry tomatoes

2 garlic cloves

1 onion

2 tbsps olive oil

1 tsp plain flour

½ tsp brown sugar

¼ tsp salt

¼ tsp black pepper

2 tsps za'atar

¼ cup (30g, 1oz) mozzarella cheese, shredded

¼ cup (30g, 1oz) Parmesan cheese, shredded

4 eggs

1 long red chilli

Basil leaves, to garnish

Preheat the oven to 190°C (375°F, Gas Mark 5).

Finely chop the tomatoes, garlic and onion.

Melt the olive oil in a large ovenproof frying pan over medium heat. Add the flour, sugar, salt and pepper and stir to combine. Cook for 1 minute, then add the tomato mixture and 1 teaspoon za'atar, continuing to stir to ensure everything is well mixed.

Allow the sauce to simmer gently for 8-10 minutes until thickened. Remove from the heat and sprinkle the two types of cheeses over the top. Crack eggs into the frying pan and then transfer it to the oven. Bake for 8 minutes until eggs are just set.

Remove from oven and sprinkle with chopped chilli and basil to serve.

Bacon Omelette Rolls

A SIMPLE AND TASTY IDEA FOR A BRUNCH PARTY, THESE BITE - SIZED
ROLLS WILL JUMP OFF THE PLATE

SERVES 4

8 eggs

1 tsp salt

1 tsp ground black pepper

1 yellow capsicum, finely diced

2 tsps olive oil

Handful parsley, chopped

½ tsp smoked paprika

½ cup (60g, 2oz) mozzarella cheese, shredded

12 slices bacon

Preheat the oven to 180°C (350°F, Gas Mark 4).

In a large bowl, combine the eggs, salt and pepper and whisk until well combined. Add the capsicum and stir to mix through.

Heat the olive oil in a frying pan over a medium-low heat. When oil is hot, pour in the egg mixture and swirl the pan around until it covers the base of it. Cover the pan with a lid and leave to cook for 4-5 minutes.

Loosen the omelette from the edges of the pan and shake out onto a chopping board or large plate. Sprinkle with parsley, paprika and mozzarella. Roll the omelette up and slice into pieces.

Wrap a piece of bacon around each roll, and hold together with a toothpick. Place the omelette rolls onto a baking tray and transfer to the oven. Cook for 25 minutes.

Guacamole Deviled Eggs

A SOPHISTICATED TAKE ON AN OLD CLASSIC THAT'S GREAT AS PART OF A BRUNCH PARTY MENU

SERVES 12

12 eggs

olive oil for frying

3 rashers bacon

3 ripe avocados

2 tbsps red onion, finely diced

Handful parsley, leaves picked

1-2 tbsps lime juice, to taste

1 serrano chilli (optional)

½ tsp salt

First, boil the eggs. Place them in a saucepan of cold water over a medium-high heat. Bring to a rapid boil and allow to cook for 3½ minutes from the point of boiling. Drain and rinse under cold water. Set aside until cool enough to peel.

Next fry the bacon. Place a splash of olive oil in a frying pan and add let the oil get nice and hot. Add the bacon and fry until crispy, around 2 minutes. Remove and set aside on paper towel to drain. When coolish, roughly chop the bacon.

Remove the peel and seed from the avocados. Place the avocados in a medium bowl and mash with a fork. Add the onion, parsley, 1 tablespoon of lime juice, chilli, if using, and salt and mix to combine. Taste and add more lime juice or salt as required.

Peel the eggs and cut in half. Scoop out the egg yolk and add it to the bowl of avocado. Lightly mash together so that the yolk is combined with the rest of the ingredients.

Place the hollowed out egg whites on a serving platter. Spoon the avocado mixture into each half and top with bacon.

HEIRLOOM TOMATOES

What is an heirloom tomato? Perhaps you've heard the term but don't really know what it means. Happily, there's an easy definition: it's a variety that has been passed down from gardener to gardener. Unlike modern hybrids, heirloom tomatoes come from seed, making them easy to share.

The main reason to choose heirloom varieties is flavour. There's no one taste, but most are prized for having a rich, old-time flavour — a far cry from those found on the supermarket aisle.

Red, yellow, gold, black: heirloom tomatoes come in a kaleidoscope of colours. They are all tasty, but yellow tomatoes have a sweeter taste than their red counterparts. Heirloom tomatoes come in a wide variety of shapes and sizes too. With names like Green Zebra, Cherokee Purple, Cosmonaut Volkov, Hillbilly and Sunray, there's an heirloom tomato for everyone. Perhaps the most famous, Brandywine is a classic strain that many rank as the best-tasting around. It features large red fruits — up to 1kg (2lb) each — and dates to the late 1800s.

COLLECTING

Collecting heirloom seed is quite easy even for a novice. The first thing to do is pick some nice ripe tomatoes. Then chop or mash them up in a jar until the jar is just less than half full. Fill up to the top with water and leave them like that for 5-6 days until the tomatoes have completely decomposed. The seeds will have sunk to the bottom. Remove them and rinse very thoroughly for several minutes under cold water until the seeds are clean. Spread them out in an even layer on a baking tray or other flat surface lined with baking paper and place them in a well-ventilated place to dry out for a further 4-5 days. Store dried seed in ziplock bags. Now you have seed ready to sow or swap with friends.

GREENIE TIPS

Many heirloom tomatoes are susceptible to cracking open on the vine. Avoid this by keeping the soil evenly moist and using an organic slow-release fertilizer.

All heirloom tomatoes grow best in a spot that has full sun (6-8 hours per day) and moist, well-drained soil rich in organic matter, such as compost.

These tomatoes weren't bred for disease resistance. To help your plants stay healthy, pick off affected leaves as soon as you see them. Discard in the rubbish, not the compost bin.

Most heirloom tomatoes grow well in large containers, making them perfect plants to grow on a sunny deck or balcony. In fact, growing them in containers can help reduce instances of disease.

Asparagus Squares

SERVES 4

2 sheets frozen puff pastry, thawed

250g (9oz) brie, thinly sliced

2 bunches asparagus

1tbsp olive oil

1 egg yolk mixed with 1tbsp milk (egg wash)

2 tbsps slivered almonds

Preheat the oven to 220°C (430°F, Gas Mark 7). Cut the pastry into four rectangular pieces. Place on a greased baking tray. Score a border of about 5mm around the edge of each one. Prick the pastry several times with a fork inside the border.

Place the brie in the middle of each piece of pastry.

Trim asparagus to fit within the pastry border, and then toss it in the olive oil to coat lightly. Season with salt and pepper. Sit in an even row on top.

Brush the pastry borders with the egg wash and place in the oven for 10 minutes, until the puff pastry is golden.

Garnish with almonds to serve.

Tomato Basil Mini Tarts

SERVES 4

1 sheet frozen puff pastry, thawed

¼ cup (30g, 1oz) Cheddar cheese, grated

4 roma tomatoes, sliced

Sea salt and ground black pepper, to taste

½ cup (60g, 2oz) Parmesan cheese, grated

Fresh basil, to garnish

Preheat the oven to 190°C (375°F, Gas Mark 5). Prepare a baking tray by greasing and lining with baking paper. Lightly flour a clean and dry work surface.

Cut the puff pastry sheet into four squares. Place the pastry squares onto the prepared baking tray.

Divide the cheese evenly among the pastry squares and then top each tart with 1-2 slices of tomato. Add salt and pepper to taste. Sprinkle each tart with 1 teaspoon of Parmesan cheese.

Place tarts in the oven and bake for 20 minutes or until pastry is golden and cheese is bubbly. Garnish with basil leaves. Set aside to cool slightly before serving.

Roasted Beetroot Tart

THIS TANGY TART IS A BEAUTIFUL, FLAVOUR-FILLED TREAT TO SHARE WITH FRIENDS

SERVES 4

SHORTCRUST PASTRY

1¾ cups (215g, 7oz) plain flour, sifted

Pinch of salt

125g (4oz) chilled butter, chopped

1 egg, lightly beaten

1 tbsp iced water

TOPPING

4 medium beetroots, peeled and cut into thin slices

½ cup (65g, 2oz) kalamata olives

Olive oil, for roasting

1 tsp balsamic vinegar

1 egg

⅔ cup (150ml, 5fl oz) double cream

200g (7oz) goat's cheese, sliced

First, make your pastry. Combine flour and salt in a large bowl. Add butter and rub into flour mixture using fingertips until fine crumbs form. Make a well in the centre of the flour mixture. Combine egg and water in a small bowl, then pour into the well. Using a round-bladed knife, or hands, stir until mixture just forms a dough.

Turn out onto a floured surface and shape into a disc. Wrap in plastic wrap and chill in the fridge for 30 minutes. Preheat the oven to 190°C (375°F, Gas Mark 5) and flour a baking tray.

On a lightly floured surface, roll the pastry into a rectangle. Place pastry on the baking tray and prick with a fork. Transfer to the oven to bake for 20 minutes. Remove from the oven and set aside to cool.

Reduce the oven temperature to 180°C (350°F, Gas Mark 4).

Next, make the topping. Place the beetroot and olives in an ovenproof dish and drizzle over the olive oil. Toss to coat with oil. Cover with foil and bake in the oven for 1 hour, until soft. Remove from the oven and set aside to cool.

Whisk the egg and cream together in a bowl.

Arrange the cheese slices in the cooled pastry case and pour over the egg mixture. Arrange the beetroot slices and olives on top. Place in the oven to bake for 20 minutes until nicely browned.

Rustic Breakfast Pizza

PEOPLE SECRETLY LOVE PIZZA FOR BREAKFAST, DON'T THEY? SHARE THE LOVE WITH THIS FRESH AND LIGHT VERSION

SERVES 2

PIZZA BASES

2 cups (250g, 8oz) baker's (or plain) flour

7g (¼ oz) sachet dry active yeast

1 tsp caster sugar

1 tsp salt

¾ cup (200ml, 7fl oz) warm water

1 tbsp olive oil, plus extra to grease

TOPPINGS

1 small zucchini, finely sliced

1 tsp olive oil

½ cup (60g, 2oz) mozzarella cheese, grated

1 tsp dried mixed herbs

3 tbsps feta cheese

4-5 green olives

Handful of rocket

Sift flour into a large mixing bowl. Stir in yeast, sugar and salt. Make a well in the centre and pour in water and oil. Bring the dough together with your hands, then turn out onto a lightly floured surface. Clean the bowl for reuse. Knead for 5 minutes by hand (or in an electric mixer with a dough hook) until the dough is smooth. Lightly grease the cleaned bowl with a little oil, then add dough and cover with a tea towel or plastic wrap. Set aside in a warm place to prove for 1 hour, until doubled in size.

Preheat oven to 240°C (465°F, Gas Mark 9). Lightly flour two baking trays.

Knock back the dough by punching it to remove air and divide into a ball. Roll dough out on a lightly floured surface to create base. Transfer to prepared baking sheets.

Reduce the oven temperature to 190°C (375°F, Gas Mark 5).

Preheat a grill pan or frying pan. Season and lightly oil the zucchini slices and grill them for 2-3 minutes on each side.

Top the pizza with cheese, grilled zucchini and herbs then place in the oven to cook for 15 minutes or until dough is golden brown and cheese is brown.

Remove from the oven and set aside to cool.

When ready to eat, top with feta cheese, olives and rocket.

Tomato Tarte Tatin

YOU CAN TASTE PARIS IN EVERY MOUTHFUL OF THIS SIMPLE, ELEGANT BRUNCH OFFERING

SERVES 6

2 tbsps butter

2 tbsps brown sugar

750g (1½ lb) cherry tomatoes

2 tbsps balsamic vinegar

2 tsps thyme leaves, chopped

Sea salt and ground black pepper

1 sheet frozen puff pastry, thawed

Basil leaves, to garnish

Preheat the oven to 200°C (400°F, Gas Mark 6) and grease a round 20cm (8in) cake tin.

Melt the butter in a large frying pan over a medium heat. Stir in the sugar and stir constantly until the sugar starts to dissolve and the mixture turns a golden brown. Then add the tomatoes and simmer for 5 minutes until tomatoes are soft but still formed.

Add vinegar to the pan and sprinkle in the thyme. Season with salt and ground pepper to taste. Cook uninterrupted for a further 2 minutes and then remove the pan from the heat.

Transfer the tomato mixture to the tin. Place the puff pastry on top of the filling and fold the excess pastry around the tomatoes.

Place in the oven to bake for 15 minutes until pastry edges are golden. Remove from the oven and set aside to cool for 5 minutes.

Invert onto a serving plate and garnish with fresh basil leaves.

Lazy
Afternoons

EVERYDAY SALADS

Every home cook should have the staple salads sorted. A simple salad provides a fresh and healthy alternative for your diners. Here are a few classics to master.

CAPRESE SALAD

The humble Caprese salad has been subject to many a modification and embellishment over the years, but simplest is best. This perfectly balanced and well-constructed salad just needs its few ingredients to be good ones: juicy, flavoursome tomatoes, soft pillowy mozzarella, fresh basil, rich tasty olive oil, good salt and cracked pepper. That's it: job done.

COLESLAW

You might remember coleslaw from your youth as a slightly gloopy mix of chewy white cabbage and carrot. The old-school dish has been swept aside by a new wave of more flavoursome alternatives, such as Asian slaw, featuring sesame oil, lime juice, peanuts, coriander and whatever else you fancy. Or a Mexian-stlye slaw featuring peppers and spices. These mayo-free coleslaws are a great alternative for the dairy-free guest.

GREEK SALAD

As with Caprese, keep your version of this classic salad to the traditional method and you won't go far wrong. A traditional Greek salad recipe includes tomato, sliced cucumber, green pepper, sliced red onion, kalamata olives and feta cheese. It is seasoned with dried oregano and salt and dressed with good quality extra virgin olive oil and a splash of red wine vinegar.

BEST DRESSED SALAD

Balance of flavours is often provided by the dressing, which should provide a combination of sweet, salty and tangy to bring out the natural flavours of the other ingredients. Here are five classic salad dressings to learn by heart so you can whip them up in no time:

QUICK RANCH DRESSING: mayonnaise and buttermilk, chives and mint.

BALSAMIC VINAIGRETTE: balsamic vinegar, good quality olive oil, salt and pepper.

BLUE CHEESE DRESSING: blue cheese, sour cream, buttermilk, mayonnaise, lemon juice.

ASIAN-STYLE DRESSING: garlic, ginger, sesame oil, soy sauce, brown sugar, rice wine vinegar.

HONEY MUSTARD DRESSING: honey, mustard, vinegar, garlic, salt and pepper.

Blackbean Salad with Lime and Coriander Dressing

AN IDEAL ACCOMPANIMENT FOR LUNCH, OR A MEAL IN ITSELF. ADD SOUR CREAM AND A SPLASH OF LIME FOR EXTRA OOMPH

SERVES 6

DRESSING

3 tbsps olive oil

2 limes, juiced

2 tbsps fresh coriander, chopped

1 tsp minced garlic

¼ tsp sea salt

SALAD

2 x 400g (14oz) cans black beans, drained and rinsed

2 cups (340g, 12oz) corn, fresh or tinned

1 red capsicum, cut into strips

2 pita breads, finely sliced

½ red onion, sliced

¹⁄₃ cup (10g, ¼oz) coriander leaves, chopped

1 tsp sea salt, to taste

Fresh ground pepper, to taste

2 avocados, sliced

In a small bowl, whisk together the olive oil, lime juice, coriander, garlic and salt. Set aside.

Place the beans, corn, capsicum, pita, red onion and coriander in a large bowl. Season with salt and pepper. (If you don't plan to eat the salad immediately, now would be a good time to transfer to an airtight container and refrigerate – for up to three days).

Pour the dressing over the salad and toss well to combine ingredients and coat thoroughly with the dressing.

Add the avocado and gently toss to combine. Serve immediately.

Grilled Chicken Grain Salad

ANCIENT GRAIN MEETS CONTEMPORARY FRESH FLAVOURS IN THIS FILLING AND HEALTHY SALAD

SERVES 4

1 eggplant, cut into pieces

2 punnets cherry tomatoes

2 tbsp olive oil

1 tbsp honey

2 tsp cumin seeds, toasted and crushed (or use ground cumin)

Salt and pepper

1 cup (170g, 6oz) quinoa, rinsed and picked through

1½ (375ml, 13fl oz) cups water

300g (10oz) chicken breast

Olive oil, for grilling

Juice of 2 limes

Zest of 1 lime

Handful fresh basil leaves, shredded

Heat oven to 200°C (400°F, Gas Mark 6). Line an oven tray with baking paper.

Drizzle and toss eggplant and whole cherry tomatoes with olive oil, honey, and cumin seeds and season with salt and pepper.

Roast until cooked through and slightly caramelised, 20-30 minutes.

Place quinoa and water in a pot along with a pinch of salt. Bring to the boil, then cover with a tight-fitting lid and cook for 15 minutes.

Meanwhile, cook the chicken. Toss chicken in olive oil and season with salt and pepper. Lay in a hot grill pan and cook for 3-4 mins each side or until cooked through. Set aside and cover with foil to keep warm.

Remove quinoa from the heat and leave to steam (with the lid on) for 8 minutes. Fluff with a fork, then set aside.

Toss quinoa, roast vegetables and lime juice and zest together, and season to taste with salt and pepper. Serve with fresh basil and a squeeze of fresh lime.

Beetroot and Feta Salad with Toasted Seeds

CRUNCHY, SALTY, EARTHY: THIS SALAD IS THE BUSINESS AND A PERFECT PARTNER TO GRILLED MEAT OR FISH

SERVES 4

ROASTED BEETROOT

3 beetroots

2 tbsps olive oil

Sea salt and cracked black pepper

TOASTED SEEDS

⅓ cup (60g, 2oz) pepitas

⅓ cup (60g, 2oz) sunflower seeds

Pinch of sea salt

DRESSING

2 tbsps olive oil

2 tbsps balsamic vinegar

1 tbsp maple syrup

Sea salt and cracked black pepper

SALAD

150g (5oz) rocket

100g (3.5oz) feta, crumbled

Preheat the oven to 180°C (350°F, Gas Mark 4). Line an oven tray with baking paper.

To prepare the beetroot, wash thoroughly then remove tops and tails with a sharp knife. Place each beetroot on one side of a piece of aluminium foil that is large enough to wrap around and create an airtight pouch. Drizzle with olive oil and season with salt and pepper, then wrap the aluminium foil over the beetroot and fold the edges to secure. Place on the baking tray and transfer to the oven to bake for 1 hour.

Place the seeds and salt in a dry frying pan over medium heat. Stir and cook for 2 minutes, watching them to make sure they don't burn.

To make the dressing place olive oil, balsamic vinegar, maple syrup and seasoning in a bowl and whisk to thoroughly combine. Set aside.

Once the beetroot is cooked, remove from the oven and allow to cool slightly so that you can work with it. When it is cool enough to be handled, remove the skin by rubbing it firmly with your hands. It should come off easily, but you could also peel to remove the skin. Cut into wedges.

To assemble the salad, divide rocket, beetroot, feta, and seeds among four serving plates. Serve with dressing.

Pearl Couscous with Roasted Vegetables

A BRIGHT AND COLOURFUL ADDITION TO YOUR BARBECUE WHICH CAN BE MADE THE DAY BEFORE AND WARMED OR SERVE CHILLED

SERVES 4

1 zucchini, chopped

2 yellow squash, chopped

3-4 garlic cloves, whole

1 carrot, sliced

1 beetroot, peeled and cut into wedges

4 Asian shallots, peeled and sliced

3 tbsps olive oil

Salt and pepper

3 cups (750ml, 24fl oz) water

1½ cups (290g, 10oz) pearl couscous

¼ cup (10g, ¼ oz) parsley, chopped

BALSAMIC DRESSING

3 tbsps balsamic vinegar

1 tbsp Dijon mustard

½ cup (125ml, 4fl oz) olive oil

Preheat the oven to 200°C (400°F, Gas Mark 6).

Place the zucchini, squash, garlic, carrot, beetroot and Asian shallots in a large baking dish. Drizzle over the olive oil and gently toss to coat. Season with salt and pepper. Transfer to the oven and roast for 35 minutes, stirring occasionally, until vegetables are soft and golden. Remove from the oven and set aside.

Place water in a medium saucepan over a high heat and bring to a boil. Add a generous pinch of salt, and stir in the couscous. Reduce heat to a simmer and continue to simmer for 12 minutes or until couscous is just tender but not mushy. Drain and rinse with cold water. Set aside.

Meanwhile, make the dressing. In a small bowl, combine the vinegar and mustard. Add the oil in a slow steady stream, whisking constantly. Season with salt and pepper to taste.

In a large bowl, combine couscous and roasted vegetables.

When ready to serve, pour dressing over the top and stir until well combined. Serve garnished with chopped parsley.

SEAFOOD

Seafood – let's say prawns, mussels and scallops – is ideally suited to sharing given the small, bite-sized nature of the ingredients. Choosing the best seafood, storing it, preparing it and cooking it can be challenging though for the inexperienced cook.

PRAWNS

Prawns are an everyday seafood and you may be familiar with buying them shelled and frozen. Buying fresh from a fishmonger is a different matter, and a good idea too, if you want the freshest options. You can buy raw (or 'green') prawns or cooked, shelled or whole. Raw prawns will have a greenish-blue hue to them, whereas cooked will be a nice bright orange.

To prepare the prawns if they are whole, remove the head then peel off the rest of the shell and you should then be able to pull the tail off easily. Make a cut down the back with a knife and remove the black 'vein' that runs along the prawn. Rinse and pat dry with paper towel. Cook immediately or store overnight in the fridge. If you are not using them today or tomorrow, freeze them. Note that some recipes in this book call for the 'tail intact'. This easy variation just requires you to peel around the tip of the tail and leave the shell on it. Generally this is for decorative purposes although in some cultures it is common to eat the whole tail (indeed the whole shell), popular for its crunchy texture.

MUSSELS

Mussels might feel a little more challenging if you are not experienced with them. As with all seafood, they should smell fresh not fishy. The shells will be bright and shiny looking. Mussels are delicate little beasts and won't keep as well as prawns. Eat them on the day of purchase (or freeze) and don't allow them to get hot during transit home from the shop: wrap in a damp cloth or keep in a cooler bag. To prepare the mussels, scrub with a firm brush to remove the beards, then rinse in cold water.

SCALLOPS

Always go for fresh scallops if you can. They don't freeze as well as other seafood and the result can be a soggy, milky, not-so-nice scallop. Choose scallops that are bright white in colour with an orange roe. They should smell fresh like the ocean and have a firm, moist texture to them. Preparation is easy: just rinse under cold water. Scallops can be seared, grilled, poached or even eaten raw if they are superior quality ones. They are a delightful and indulgent treat for your dinners.

Citrusy Spicy Scallops

SUCCULENT AND TANGY, THESE SCALLOPS MAKE FOR AN EASY AND IMPRESSIVE DISH

SERVES 4

8 scallops

2 tbsps vegetable oil

2 garlic cloves, finely chopped

Small piece ginger, finely chopped

1 orange, zested and juiced

½ lime, juiced

¼ cup (60ml, 2fl oz) Thai sweet chilli sauce

1 red chilli, seeded and sliced (optional - for extra spice)

¼ cup (25g, 1oz) spring onion, sliced

If you've bought scallops in the shell, remove them and retain the shell. Gently clean the scallops under running water and pat dry with paper towel.

Heat a tablespoon of the oil in a large frying pan over a medium-high heat. Add garlic and ginger and fry for 2 minutes or until lightly golden. Be careful not to overcook the garlic. It will burn quickly and taste sour.

Add the orange zest, orange and lime juice, sweet chilli sauce, extra chilli, if using, and spring onions to the pan and cook for a further 2 minutes until ingredients are soft and well combined. Remove from the heat and place in a small bowl.

Using the same frying pan, heat the rest of the oil. When it's nice and hot, add the scallops to the pan in a single layer and sear on the first side for 90 seconds, turn over carefully and cook on the other side for 1 minute.

Pour the reserved sauce into the pan and gently turn the scallops to coat in the sauce. Be quick because you don't want to overcook the scallops – they will become rubbery.

Return the scallops to the shell, if using, or place in a serving dish. Spoon additional sauce from the pan over the scallops and serve.

Chargrilled Tandoori Prawns

PACKED FULL OF FLAVOUR, THESE SPICY PRAWNS ARE A
GREAT ADDITION TO YOUR AFTERNOON BARBECUE

SERVES 6

18 large green prawns

3 tbsps vegetable oil

1 tsp ground coriander

1 tsp ground cumin

½ tsp ground turmeric

1 tsp cayenne

1 tbsp garam masala

1 tbsp sweet paprika

1 cup (250g, 8oz)
plain yoghurt

2 tbsps lemon juice

4 garlic cloves, minced

1 tsp salt

1 small piece ginger,
minced

Prepare the prawns first, by removing the head and outer shell but leaving the tails intact. Devein and then rinse under cool water. Pat dry with paper towel.

Heat the oil in a small frying pan over medium heat. Add the coriander, cumin, turmeric, cayenne, garam masala and paprika and fry, stirring often, until aromatic. Set aside to cool completely.

In a small bowl, combine the oil mixture with the yoghurt, then mix in the lemon juice, garlic, salt and ginger.

Spoon over the marinade and rub it well into the prawns using your fingers. Cover and refrigerate for 3 hours (or overnight if time allows).

Heat the grill or barbecue to a high setting.

Remove prawns from the fridge and shake off excess marinade.

Put the prawns on grill and cook for 2-3 minutes each side until golden on the outside (a few blackened bits are nice too) and cooked through.

Allow to rest for a few minutes before serving.

Coconut Roti and Onion Sambol

TRY THIS SRI LANKAN STYLE ROTI AND SAMBOL COMBO FOR AN INTERESTING ACCOMPANIMENT TO BARBECUED FISH AND MEAT

SERVES 6

ONION SAMBOL

Olive oil, for frying

1 large red onion, chopped

3-4 dried red chillies or 2-3 tbsps red chilli powder, to taste

Salt to taste

Juice of 1 small lemon

ROTI

1 cup (90g, 3oz) freshly grated coconut or desiccated coconut

Salt, to taste

1 tbsp vegetable oil

3 cups (375g, 12oz) plain flour, sifted

1 cup (250ml, 8fl oz) cold water

Olive oil, for frying

1 onion, finely chopped

First of all, make the onion sambol.

Heat the olive oil in a large frying pan and add the onions. Saute for a few minutes, then add the red chillies and salt and fry for a further minutes.

Transfer the onion mix to a high-speed blender. Add lemon juice and blitz until a coarse paste forms.

Next make your roti (coconut pancakes).

If using desiccated coconut, soak in water for 20 minutes, then drain. Combine the coconut, salt and vegetable oil with the flour and mix well. Gradually add the water, a little at a time until it forms a dough, not too soft but a stiff and workable dough.

Heat the olive oil in a small frying pan. Fry the onion on a medium heat for 5 minutes or until soft. Gently combine with the dough.

Roll the dough into balls. Use a piece of lightly greased silver foil to flatten each dough ball into a round shape.

Heat olive oil in a heavy-based frying pan over a medium-high heat. Place a dough ball in the pan and cook on each side for 3 minutes or until golden brown.

Mango Mint Wraps

SERVES 4

MANGO DRESSING

½ spring onion, finely chopped

½ mango, peeled and roughly chopped

2 tsps lime juice

Pinch cayenne pepper

WRAPS

4 soft flatbreads

2 mangos, peeled and diced

Handful fresh mint leaves

First make the dressing. If you have a food processor, now would be a good time to use it. If not, you can make the dressing by hand instead. Place the spring onion and mango in the bowl and process until thick and smooth. Next add the lime juice and cayenne pepper and combine everything well.

To assemble the wraps, spread the mango dressing in the centre of each of the flatbreads and top with the diced mango and mint leaves. Roll up each flatbread and slice in half. Tie each half with string or wrap in paper to serve.

Spicy Mango Slaw

SERVES 2

DRESSING

2 limes, juiced

1 tsp sambal oelek

2 tsps peanut oil

½ tsp maple syrup

¼ tsp fish sauce

SALAD

⅓ red cabbage, shredded

1 mango, peeled and diced

¼ red onion, thinly sliced

1 carrot, peeled and thinly sliced

1 bird's-eye chilli, thinly sliced

Handful of dill, chopped

Handful of mint, chopped

First make the dressing. Put the ingredients into a small glass jar with a sealable lid. Shake until well combined.

Place the salad ingredients into a large salad bowl, and pour a good splash of the dressing over the top. Toss to combine and add more dressing to taste.

MANGO

Man go crazy for this sweet fruit, and women seem to like it too. It provides a great counterbalance to seafood, but use it sparingly according to the dish you are cooking. Mango can overpower delicate scallops, but it gives a needed lift to more neutral fish and seafood.

BARBECUE GODS AND GODESSES

All hail the summer barbie! There's nothing quite like a long, lazy Sunday afternoon barbecue with friends and family. The best ones simmer on past sundown as fairy lights start to replace sunshine and mocktails morph into cocktails. But how do you put on a sizzling barbecue everyone will enjoy?

PREPARE

Make it easy on yourself and get everything ready in advance. Make your marinades and get your meat and fish coated in it the day before – more flavour, less fuss. Make the dressings a day before too.

Don't forget about vegetables! Snags and chops are a firm favourite. However, a sweet potato slow-cooked on the barbie in a foil packet will be a melt-in-the-mouth accompaniment to the meal. Likewise, a chargrilled corn cob is a sweet and smoky hit as a an accompaniment. Pineapple on the barbecue is always a hit, with adults and kids alike. There's a recipe for it in this book on page 90. But don't neglect other desserts. It's amazing what you can cook on the barbecue: everyone will love caramelised bananas or strawberries freshly grilled.

Then, of course there's the golden 'cooking times'. Nobody wants a rubber prawn or a tough old steak, so put the margaritas on hold (for yourself that is!) until you've done your stuff at the hotplate.

COOKING GUIDELINES

PRAWNS: 2-3 minutes each side (depending on size)

CHOPS: 4 minutes each side

THIN STEAK: 1½ mins (rare), 2½ mins (medium), 3½ mins (well done)

THICK STEAK: 2½ mins (rare), 4½ mins (medium), 5½ mins (well done)

OTHER TIPS

Have a spare gas bottle.
Have plenty of clean glasses and back ups.
Napkins are a must.

DRINKS

It goes without saying that you're going to need ice, ice and more ice. Check beforehand that you have enough big containers and if you don't the bath tub might be an option.

Why not make a great big punch such as rosehip with plenty of cut up fruit like pineapple and strawberry and mint leaves too. Serve in a large vat on the main table, and adults and kids can help themselves. The adults can add a dash of something stronger if they like, but the punch can serve as the base for everybody's drink. Then all you need is jugs or bottles of water.

Sticky Pineapple Rings

SERVES 4

1 pineapple

6-8 tbsps honey (or maple syrup)

To peel the pineapple, top and tail it so that you have a flat surface. Place the flat end on a chopping board and using a sharp knife slice off the skin in pieces from top to bottom. Easy! If you have a corer, use it to cut out the core so that you can slice the pineapple into 6-8 rings, depending on its size. Otherwise cut the slices into wedges and trim off the core from each wedge.

If using a grill, place the pineapple on the double thickness of aluminum foil and drizzle a tablespoon of honey over each piece. Just use a plate for this if you are barbecuing. Cover to keep the flies away and set aside for 30 minutes or so.

When you are ready to cook, preheat the grill or barbecue to a medium heat.

Wrap the pineapple pieces securely in foil and transfer to the grill to cook for 20 minutes, or simply place on the barbecue as they are (no need for foil).

Serve warm; great with sweet or savoury dishes.

BBQ Basting Sauce

SERVES 6 (3 CUPS)

3 cups (750ml, 24fl oz) tomato sauce

1 cup (250ml, 8fl oz) apple cider vinegar

½ cup (180g, 6oz) molasses

2 tbsps Worcestershire sauce

1 cup (250ml, 8fl oz) water

1 tbsp white sugar

1 tbsp paprika

1 tbsp onion powder

1 tbsp mustard powder

1 tsp garlic powder

1 tsp salt

½ tsp ground black pepper

¼-½ tsp cayenne pepper

Place ingredients in a medium-sized saucepan over a high heat and bring to the boil. Reduce heat to medium-low and let the sauce simmer away until it has reduced by around a third. This should take around 30 minutes.

Allow the sauce to cool to room temperature before using. This sauce is great for basting chicken or red meat before grilling or barbecuing.

HALLOUMI

Halloumi is a winner on the barbecue. It's just so easy.
Cut into thick slices and rub with a small amount
of olive oil. Place on the grill for around 1 minute
either side until golden brown on the outside and
just soft inside. Squeeze with lemon juice to serve.

Slow-Cooked Pork Ribs

A SET - AND - FORGET SPECIAL WHERE ALL THE WORK IS DONE THE NIGHT BEFORE, SO YOU CAN ENJOY THE COMPANY OF YOUR GUESTS

SERVES 4

2 sides (1¼ kg, 3lb 4oz) baby pork ribs

1 cup (250ml, 8fl oz) BBQ basting sauce (see recipe page 90)

Rosemary, to garnish

Place the ribs in a container large enough to stack them one on top of the other.

Pour the basting sauce over the ribs and turn to coat, rubbing in with your fingers.

Cover with plastic wrap and transfer to the fridge to marinate overnight.

Preheat the oven to 150°C (300°F, Gas Mark 2).

Remove ribs from the fridge and set aside half of the marinade.

Place the ribs with the other half of the marinade in a baking tray. Transfer to the oven and bake, turning the ribs frequently, for 2 hours, or until the meat is tender.

Heat a grill pan over a high heat. Finish the ribs by glazing each side for 3-4 minutes.

Remove the ribs and cut each side into individual pieces.

Bring the reserved marinade to a boil and serve on the side.

Sticky Chinese Chicken Wings

A SURE WINNER FOR ANY AFTERNOON BARBECUE, THESE CHICKEN WINGS ARE A HIT WITH KIDS AND ADULTS

SERVES 6

MARINADE

½ tsp sesame oil

2 tbsps lemon juice (or white vinegar)

2 tbsps Chinese cooking wine (or sherry)

¼ cup (60ml, 2fl oz) soy sauce

2 tbsps brown sugar or honey

¼ cup (60ml, 2fl oz) tomato ketchup

2 tbsps hoisin sauce

2 tbsps oyster sauce

2 tbsps sambal oelek

4 garlic cloves, minced

1 tbsp ginger, finely chopped or minced

½ tsp five-spice powder

CHICKEN WINGS

12 chicken wings

2 tbsps sesame seeds

Combine the ingredients for the marinade in a large bowl.

Add the wings and turn to coat well. Cover and set aside for 10 minutes (or up to 1 hour if you need to).

Preheat the oven to 180°C (350°F, Gas Mark 4), and line a baking tray with greaseproof paper. Sprinkle the sesame seeds onto a clean plate.

Shake the excess marinade off wings, reserving the marinade to use later. Place the wings in an even layer on the baking tray.

Place the wings into the oven to bake for 45 minutes until the meat is very tender and the skin has developed a deep reddish brown and is starting to blacken at the edges. Using the reserved marinade, baste the wings a few times during cooking.

Scatter sesame seeds over the top of the wings before serving.

Balinese Chicken Satay

FLAVOUR, TEXTURE, PRESENTATION: THESE LITTLE SKEWERS
HAVE ALL THE INGREDIENTS FOR A GREAT LUNCH

SERVES 4

⅓ cup (80ml, 3fl oz) coconut milk

4 garlic cloves, crushed

1 tbsp turmeric

2 tbsps fresh coriander, chopped (plus more to garnish)

2 tbsps brown sugar

2 tbsps fish sauce

½ tsp sea salt

1kg (2lb) boneless skinless chicken tenders, pounded extra thin

PEANUT SAUCE

1½ cups (375ml, 13fl oz) coconut milk

¼ cup (60ml, 2fl oz) Thai red curry paste

¾ cup (185ml, 6fl oz) smooth peanut butter

½ tbsp salt

¾ cup (165g, 6oz) white sugar

2 tbsps apple cider vinegar

½ cup (125ml, 4fl oz) water

¼ cup (30g, 1oz) peanuts, crushed

Combine the coconut milk, garlic, turmeric, coriander, brown sugar, fish sauce and salt in a small bowl.

Arrange the chicken on a plate or dish in a single layer and pour the marinade over the top. Cover with cling film and place in the fridge to marinate for a minimum of 1 hour, or overnight.

To prepare the peanut sauce place all the ingredients in a small saucepan over a medium heat. Whisking to combine, bring the sauce to a gentle simmer. Cook for 5 minutes, stirring constantly to thicken the sauce and ensure it doesn't stick and burn. Remove from heat and set aside for 10 minutes before serving. If it gets a little thick, add warm water to thin it out to your desired consistency.

Preheat grill to a medium heat.

Remove chicken from the fridge and bring to room temperature. Thread the meat lengthwise onto metal or bamboo skewers.

Place the chicken skewers on the prepared grill and allow to cook uninterrupted for 3-5 minutes. Turn the meat and grill for a further 2 minutes, until the chicken is just cooked through.

Serve with peanut sauce.

Grapefruit Cocktail

SERVES 2

Handful of ice

2 shots vodka

⅓ cup (80ml, 3fl oz) pink grapefruit juice

1 tbsp honey

½ pink grapefruit, to garnish

First of all, put your glasses in the freezer to chill.

Place the ice cubes into a cocktail shaker, or if you don't have one just use a bottle or jar with a tight fitting lid.

Pour in the vodka, grapefruit juice and honey.

Do your cocktail moves until the shaker looks frosty, usually around 5 or 6 seconds.

Strain into your prepared glasses, garnish with a grapefruit wedge and enjoy.

Stormy Ginger Beer

SERVES 1

Handful of ice

¼ fresh lime

⅓ cup (80ml, 3fl oz) ginger beer

1 shot dark or spiced rum

Fill a serving glass with ice. Squeeze a slice of lime over the ice. Next, pour in the ginger beer. Finally add the rum and finish with a lime wedge on the side of your glass. Sit back and let the conversation flow!

White Chocolate Panna Cotta with Citrus Fruits

SMOOTH, CREAMY, SWEET AND TANGY, THIS IS A DESSERT THAT WILL NOT DISAPPOINT

SERVES 6

2 gelatin leaves (or 1½ tsps powdered gelatin)

1¼ cups (310ml, 10fl oz) double cream (48% milk fat)

1¼ cups (310ml, 10fl oz) cream

5 tbsps caster sugar

1 tsp vanilla extract

100g (3½ oz) good-quality white chocolate

1 pink grapefruit, peeled and segmented

1 grapefruit, peeled and segmented

Mint leaves, to garnish

First prepare the gelatin leaves by soaking in cold water according to the instructions on the packet. Squeeze out excess water before using.

Put the creams, sugar and vanilla in a saucepan over a medium heat and cook, stirring constantly, until the sugar has dissolved. Next add the chocolate and stir once or twice. Remove from the heat and allow the chocolate to dissolve.

Add the gelatin to the cream mixture (if you are using powdered, just sprinkle it in now) and stir gently until combined. Set aside to cool slightly and then spoon the mixture into serving glasses. Cover and place in the fridge for at least 4 hours so that the pannacotta sets, before serving.

Top generously with grapefruit segments to serve and garnish with mint leaves.

No-Bake Tim Tam Cheesecake with Chocolate Sauce

THE MIGHTY TIM TAM STEALS THE SHOW IN THIS EASY, CREAMY, EVERYONE-WILL-LOVE IT CHEESECAKE

SERVES 8

CRUST

60g (2oz) butter, melted

20 Tim Tam biscuits, finely crushed

FILLING

680g (1½ lb) cream cheese, room temperature

½ cup (80g, 3oz) icing sugar

2 cups (500ml, 1pt) whipping cream

1 tsp vanilla extract

1 cup (185g, 6oz) Tim Tam crumbs (about 10 Tim Tams broken up into small pieces)

CHOCOLATE SAUCE

50g (2oz) dark chocolate (at least 70% cocoa)

2 tbsps butter

½ cup (125ml, 4fl oz) double cream

1 tbsp caster sugar

First, make the cheesecake crust. Place the butter in a large bowl and pour over the crushed Tim Tams. Give the mixture a good stir to ensure all the biscuits are well coated in butter.

Press the crust mixture into the bottom of a springform pan and transfer to the fridge to chill for 15 minutes.

To make the filling, place the cream cheese and icing sugar in a mixing bowl and beat well until the mixture is thick and creamy. Now add the whipping cream and vanilla and continue to mix until all the ingredients are well combined. You can use an electric mixer or even a wooden spoon to combine the ingredients. At the end, gently stir in the Tim Tam crumbs.

Remove the crust from the fridge and spoon in the filling. Smooth over the top with a spatula and then cover with cling film and return to the fridge.

To make the chocolate sauce, place a saucepan of water on a medium-high heat and bring to a simmer. Put the chocolate in a heatproof bowl and place this bowl on top of the simmering water. Stir until the chocolate melts, then add the other ingredients and cook for 1 minute, stirring continuously, until all ingredients are well combined and the sauce is glossy.

Serve cheesecake with chocolate sauce, and extra whipped cream, if you like.

If you don't have Tim Tams, you can use other chocolate biscuits with a cream filling, such as Oreos, to make this cheesecake.

Mini Pavlovas with Berry Jam

THESE MOUTHFULS OF CREAMY, FRUITY GOODNESS FILLED WITH GOOEY MERINGUE WILL BE A PERFECT TREAT FOR YOUR GUESTS

SERVES 8

4 egg whites

1¼ cups (275g, 10oz) caster sugar, sifted

½ tsp white vinegar

1 tbsp cornflour

TO SERVE

2 cups (500ml, 1pt) whipped cream

Berry jam

Fresh berries

Preheat oven to 200°C (390°F, Gas Mark 6) and line a baking tray with greaseproof paper. Draw circles onto the paper about the size you'd like your mini pavlovas to be.

Using an electric mixer, beat the egg whites on a medium setting until soft peaks form.

With the machine running on high, add the sugar all at once and beat the mixture for 1-2 minutes until glossy. Continue to beat on high until the mixture thickens. When dropped back into the bowl, the mixture should sit on top rather than collapse back into itself.

Reduce the mixer to a medium speed and add the vinegar. Beat for 10 seconds and then remove the bowl from the mixer.

Sift cornflour over the egg white mixture and lightly combine with a spatula.

Spoon meringue into the circles on the baking paper and shape with a spatula or knife, quickly creating a few peaks around the edges. Use the back of a spoon to create an indent in the centre.

Place the tray in the middle of the oven and turn the temperature down to 120°C (250°F, Gas Mark ½). Bake for 1 hr and 30 minutes checking before the end that the pavlova has not browned. When cooked, the crust should be firm and the inside soft and marshmallowy.

Cool to room temperature and decorate with whipped cream, berry jam and berries.

Note: For a quick and easy version, you can buy pre-made mini pavlova shells at most supermarkets ready for your own toppings.

SIMPLY PRETTY

It's a known fact that we eat first with our eyes, but often appearance is not the focus of our efforts as cooks. When cooking for others, it's arguably more important, as we want to present our food as we wish to present ourselves. Luckily, it's often the simplest of touches that can transform an easy dish into something special.

When you are creating a plate to share, consider these ideas for making it look beautiful.

EDIBLE DECORATION

Go to the trendiest of cafes for brunch these days and you might find a dandelion, wild sorrel leaf or wild fennel flowers, or even a pansy, adorning your eggs. Why not try this with your bring-a-plate choice? Take a few flowers with you and scatter them around the plate or table, and you'll have your friends intrigued.

Can you really eat a pansy and what does it taste like? The flowers are very mild, flavourless almost, but the stems, which you can also eat, are grassy. Nasturtiums are another great option. These peppery-tasting flowers are packed with vitamin C, so they are not just a pretty face. Marigolds are sensational to look at and will brighten up any plate, but they do have a strong, spicy taste that is not to everybody's liking.

PRESENTATION

A carefully considered presentation can transform your dip from everyday to 'no way!' Try serving it in the original vegetable from whence it came. For example, serve your baba ganoush in a scooped-out eggplant, or serve your spiced pumpkin dip in a hollowed-out pumpkin. These little touches will provide a fun talking point for your friends.

Something as simple as popcorn can be made special by presenting it nicely. See if you can purchase little striped cardboard containers. Stack high with popcorn and cover with cellophane tied up with string to create a deluxe popcorn experience.

Muffins and cupcakes are a bring-a-plate staple. A lovely way to present them is in a recycled egg container — one that you've decorated at home first, of course. Another option is a plastic wrap box covered in wrapping paper of your choice.

Don't forget about jars, labels and string! A brown-paper label — or something more colourful if that's more your style — is a stylish and practical way to present your offering. You could even consider adding basic ingredients on the lavel, or allergy information such as 'gluten-free' or 'dairy-free' if appropriate. A thoughtful and lovely way to offer food to your friends and family.

Braided Bread with Wild Garlic and Spinach

A CONTEMPORARY AND STYLISH TWIST ON GARLIC BREAD THAT'S SURE TO DELIGHT YOUR FRIENDS

SERVES 6

FILLING

1 bulb wild garlic (use ordinary garlic if you can't find wild)

1 bunch spinach

1 cup (125g, 4oz) mozzarella cheese, grated

Handful olives, pitted

DOUGH

2 eggs

1 tbsp sugar

2 tbsps oil

½ tsp salt

¼ cup (60ml, 2fl oz) warm water

1 cup (125g, 4oz) plain flour

½ cup (60g, 2oz) whole wheat flour

1 tsp active dry yeast

Sesame seeds to garnish

First, prepare the filling. Preheat the oven to 200°C (400°F, Gas Mark 6). Rub garlic bulb with olive oil and then place in a small covered casserole dish and transfer to the oven to roast for 35 minutes. Remove and set aside until cooled slightly, then squeeze each clove to remove the roasted garlic. Place garlic in a large bowl.

Meanwhile, cook the spinach by blanching it for 30 seconds in a large saucepan of boiling water. Drain and set aside to cool slightly. When cool, remove as much water as you can by squeezing it through a potato ricer (if you have one) or use a clean tea towel. Add it to the bowl with the garlic, and then add the cheese and olives. Stir to combine.

Next, make the dough. In a small bowl, whisk together 1 egg, sugar, oil, salt and warm water. In a medium bowl, mix together the flours and the yeast. Pour the egg mixture into the dry ingredients, and mix to form a rough dough.

Place the dough on a lightly floured surface and knead for about 5 minutes until the dough springs back to the touch. Transfer to an oiled bowl and roll to coat in oil. Cover with a clean towel and place in a warm place to rise for 1 hour.

Preheat the oven to 175°C (350°F, Gas Mark 4), and line a baking sheet with greaseproof paper.

Transfer your risen dough to the baking sheet, and stretch it diagonally into a rectangle that almost fills the sheet. Place your filling in a line down the centre of the dough, leaving plenty of space on each side, and an inch or so of space top and bottom.

Now you need to cut strips into the dough that remains on each side of your filling. Starting at the top, cut uniform strips on the diagonal downwards from the outside (about 2cm/1in wide).

To braid the bread fold one strip over the filling, and then overlap with a strip on the other side. Repeat until you reach the end. Before folding the final strip, fold up the dough that remains at each end over the filling. Cover with the final strips.

Beat the remaining egg in a small bowl, and brush the top of the bread with the egg wash. Sprinkle with sesame seeds, and transfer to the oven to bake for 30 minutes or until golden.

Cinnamon Rolls

BE THE BAKER'S DELIGHT AT YOUR SOCIAL GATHERING WITH THESE NOT - AS - DIFFICULT - AS - YOU - THINK CINNAMON ROLLS

SERVES 12

DOUGH

1 cup (250ml, 8fl oz) warm milk

2 eggs

160g (6oz) butter, cubed

6 cups (750g, 1½ lb) plain flour

1¾ tsp salt

½ cup (110g, 4oz) sugar

2½ tsps instant yeast

FILLING

85g (3oz) butter, room temperature

1 cup (155g, 5oz) brown sugar, packed

3 tbsps ground cinnamon

ICING

6 tbsps cream cheese, softened

55g (2oz) butter, room temperature

1 cup (155g, 5oz) icing sugar

½ tsp vanilla extract

Flaked almonds, to serve

Mix together dough ingredients, by hand or in an electric mixer, and knead to make a smooth, soft dough.

Place the dough in a lightly oiled bowl, turning to grease all sides. Cover the bowl with a tea towel, and let the dough rise for 1 hour or until nearly doubled in size.

Transfer dough to a lightly greased work surface, and roll into a 40 x 55cm (16 x 21in) rectangle. Spread butter over the dough using a spatula.

Mix brown sugar and cinnamon together, and sprinkle liberally and evenly over the dough.

Roll the dough into a log and cut log into 12 slices.

Place the rolls in a lightly greased 23 x 33cm (9 x 13in) baking tin. Cover and leave for 30 minutes or until almost double in size.

Preheat the oven to 200°C (400°F, Gas Mark 6).

Uncover the rolls, and place in the oven to bake for 15 minutes or until golden brown.

Meanwhile, beat together cream cheese, butter, icing sugar and vanilla in a small bowl.

Remove rolls from the oven and allow to cool until warm. Spread on the icing, scatter with flaked almonds and serve.

Cheese and Chutney Mini Muffins

CHEWY AND GOOEY THESE LITTLE MOUTHFULS ARE A GUARANTEED CROWD PLEASER

SERVES 6

2 cups (250g, 8oz) self-raising flour

1 tsp baking powder

²/₃ cup (80g, 3oz) Parmesan, finely grated

Salt and cracked black pepper

¾ cup (185ml, 6fl oz) milk

½ cup (125ml, 4fl oz) olive oil

2 lightly beaten eggs

2 tbsps tomato chutney

Extra cheese and chopped parsley, to serve

Preheat oven to 190°C (375°F, Gas Mark 5), and grease a 12-hole mini muffin tray.

Sift flour and baking powder into a large mixing bowl. Add the Parmesan, salt and pepper and stir to combine. In another bowl, combine the wet ingredients (milk, olive oil and eggs) and bring them together with a fork or whisk. Add the liquid ingredients into the flour mixture. Gently combine to create a dough.

Using a teaspoon, drop balls of mixture in each muffin hole, so that the mixture comes up about three-quarters of the way, leaving room for the chutney. Make a little well in the centre of each muffin and spoon the tomato chutney into each hole.

Place in the oven to bake for 10-12 minutes until golden on top and cooked through (test to see if a skewer inserted in the centre comes out clean).

Remove from the oven and allow to cool in the tin for 5 minutes, before turning out onto a wire rack.

Serve garnished with extra cheese and chopped herbs.

ARANCINI BALLS

Like gelati, arancini are Sicilian in origin, although you'll find them nowadays across Italy and indeed the world. They're a staple canape on party menus.

If you happen to be in Sicily's capital, Palermo, in December you might be lucky enough to stumble upon the Festival of Saint Lucia, where the city streets come alive with street-food vendors. Pasta and bread are not allowed at this festival so here you'll find arancini balls of all shapes, sizes and flavours, freshly cooked, dripping with hot oil and served in neat conical packages. You might even be lucky enough to find the sweet version made with sugar and cacao. (Try this at home with Nutella in the middle for a kid-friendly treat every now and again.)

Arancini balls are traditionally stuffed with a combination of meat, mozzarella cheese and peas. Most often they are round in shape, and vary from large to mini 'mouthful size', but the traditional shape in Sicily is conical. These days there is really no standard flavour combination for arancini. There are some popular options, such as mushroom, blue cheese and eggplant, but the best flavour combination for arancini is the one you like best.

When making arancini there are a few elements to consider in the pursuit of the perfect result.

The first, of course, is the rice. Most would recommend using Arborio, the undisputed heart of risotto, but others make the case for the even shorter grain of sushi rice. It's a nice touch to add a little saffron to your risotto rice. This will give it a sweet golden hue, reminiscent of the 'little oranges' of the Italian word *arancini.*

Next up you'll want to consider how to achieve the goodly mix of crunchy on the outside and moist and creamy on the inside. Risotto, especially chilled risotto, can have a tendency to dry out. One way to moisten it up again is to add a bechamel sauce after you have made the risotto but before you chill it.

Crunch is created mostly by the choice of crumb and also by the way that you fry the arancini. To crumb your arancini, you have a choice of traditional breadcrumbs (bought from a store), home-made breadcrumbs (which you can make to your desired consistency) or the Japanese breadcrumbs, panko, which are thicker, resulting in a more cornflake-ish texture. Before rolling in breadcrumbs, gently roll the balls in flour. Deep fry in plenty of oil at a high temperature and remember not to over-crowd the frying pan. Frying in batches and draining on paper towel will give the best result.

Don't forget that if you have leftover risotto, arancini is an ideal way to use it up. Arancini balls give risotto a new lease of life and one which involves crunchiness and gooey cheese inside. So good.

Sage Mushroom Arancini

CRUNCHY, GOOEY GOODNESS. TRY THE FLAVOUR COMBINATION ON THE NEXT PAGE TOO

SERVES 12

180g (6oz) butter

3 onions, finely chopped

450g (15oz) button mushrooms, thinly sliced

3 garlic cloves, finely chopped

2¼ cups (360g, 12oz) Arborio rice

9 cups (2.25L, 72 fl oz) chicken stock

1½ cup (180g, 6oz) Parmesan, grated

¾ cup (30g, ¾ oz) sage, chopped

1 egg, whisked

4 cups (500g, 16oz) breadcrumbs

Olive oil for frying

Heat the butter in a large saucepan over a medium-high heat. Add the onions, mushrooms and garlic and fry for 5-6 minutes, or until the onions are soft.

Add the rice to the pan and stir to coat the grains, before beginning to add the stock. First add a full cup of stock and simmer for a few minutes until absorbed. Continue this process until the stock has all been absorbed and the rice is cooked. Then stir through the Parmesan and herbs. Set aside to cool.

When mixture is cool, roll into small balls.

Place the whisked egg in a medium sized bowl, and place the breadcrumbs on a clean work surface. Working one at a time, dip a ball into the egg and then roll it in the breadcrumbs.

Add oil to a frying pan to a depth of 2½ cm (1in) and heat over medium-high heat. When the oil is shimmering, add the risotto balls (in batches so that you don't crowd the frying pan) and fry, turning occasionally to ensure even cooking. Add more of the olive oil as needed. When brown and crunchy, remove from the pan and place on paper towel to drain off excess oil.

Note: To make the tomato arancini on page 124, follow the steps outlined in this recipe from the second paragraph onwards.

Tomato Arancini

SERVES 6

Butter, for frying

1½ onions, finely sliced

¼ leek, finely sliced

1 garlic clove, finely chopped

1 cup (200g, 7oz) cherry tomatoes, halved

1 carrot, peeled, grated

2 tbsps tomato puree

1½ cups (230g, 6oz) Arborio rice

2 cups (500ml, 1pt) vegetable stock (at room temperature)

½ cup (60g, 2oz) Parmesan, grated

1 tbsp parsley, finely chopped

1 egg, whisked

1 cup (125g, 4oz) breadcrumbs

Olive oil for frying

Heat the butter in a large saucepan over a medium-high heat. Add the onion, leek and garlic and fry for 6 minutes, or until the onions are soft. Add the tomatoes and carrot and cook, stirring, for a further 5 minutes. Add the tomato puree and stir a couple of times. Now follow the recipe on page 122 from the second paragraph.

Arrabiata Sauce

SERVES 6

1 tsp olive oil

½ large onion, finely diced

½ red chilli, finely diced

1 tsp cayenne pepper

½ tsp smoked paprika

⅔ cup (150ml, 5fl oz) balsamic vinegar

1 tbsp caster sugar

3 x 400g (14oz) cans chopped tomatoes

1 bay leaf

½ tsp Tabasco

1 garlic clove, minced

Pour a splash of olive oil in a frying pan over medium heat. Add onions and chilli and fry for 5 minutes until soft, then add cayenne pepper, smoked paprika, balsamic vinegar and sugar and stir. Cook for a further 2-3 minutes until the vinegar begins to thicken, then add chopped tomatoes, bay leaf, Tabasco and garlic. Stir well. Leave to simmer on a low heat for at least 2 hours or until it reaches a thick consistency. Season to taste with salt and pepper.

MARINATING MUSHROOMS

Mushrooms are fantastic for soaking up flavours which makes them perfect for marinating. Marinating doesn't have to be a chore, it can actually be simple and fast. Just cook your mushrooms in salted water until they start to soften, drain the water thoroughly and mix through your chosen marinade. Now place the mushrooms in an airtight container in the fridge overnight and voila! They are ready to eat.

Individual Autumn Tartlets

EARTHY, MEATY, WILD MUSHROOMS MEET BUTTERY, SOFT PASTRY IN THESE TASTY TARTLETS

SERVES 6

SHORTCRUST PASTRY

1¾ cups (215g, 7oz) plain flour, sifted

Pinch of salt

125g (4oz) chilled butter, chopped

1 egg, lightly beaten

1 tbsp iced water

FILLING

½ tsp salt

1 tsp olive oil

1 tbsp butter

3-4 leeks, chopped, white part only

½ bunch thyme, leaves picked

Pinch of salt

450g (1lb) wild mushrooms (such as chanterelle), chopped

1 cup (250ml, 8fl oz) thickened cream

2 eggs, beaten

¼ tsp pepper

½ cup (60g, 2oz) Cheddar or Swiss cheese, grated

First, make your pastry. Combine flour and salt in a large bowl. Add butter and rub into flour mixture using fingertips until fine crumbs form. Make a well in the centre of the flour mixture. Combine egg and water in a small bowl, then pour into the well. Using a round-bladed knife, or hands, stir until mixture just forms a dough.

Preheat oven to 220°C (425°F, Gas Mark 7) and grease 6 springform tartlet tins.

Turn pastry onto a floured surface and roll into a circle. Press pastry into tartlet tins and trim edges. Prick the bottom of each pastry shell with a fork. Line the pastry with baking paper, and fill with baking weights, such as dried beans, then place in the oven and blind bake for 20 minutes. Remove the beans and paper and return to the oven to bake for a further 10 minutes. Transfer from the oven to a wire rack to cool.

Meanwhile, melt butter in a large frying pan over medium heat. Add leeks, thyme leaves and a pinch of salt. Cover and cook over medium-low heat for 5 minutes, until leeks have softened. Add mushrooms and cook for a further 5 minutes until soft.

Combine cream, eggs, pepper, leeks and mushrooms in a medium bowl. Pour mixture into pastry shells and sprinkle with cheese.

Place in the oven and bake for 30 minutes, until filling is set and cheese is golden on top. Cool on a wire rack.

Stuffed Cabbage Rolls

JUICY AND SUBSTANTIAL, THESE VEGETARIAN CABBAGE ROLLS WILL HAVE YOUR GUESTS LICKING THEIR LIPS AND ASKING FOR MORE

SERVES 6

1 cup (155g, 4oz) wild rice (or brown rice)

1 tsp olive oil

1 onion, finely chopped

3 garlic cloves, minced

225g (8oz, ½ lb) mushrooms, finely chopped

Pinch of chilli flakes

2 tsps thyme

¼ tsp pepper

½ tsp salt

1 head savoy cabbage, leaves separated

SAUCE

400g (14oz) passata

⅓ cup (80ml, 3fl oz) tomato paste

2 tsps basil

½ tsp salt

½ tsp smoked paprika

1 cup (250ml, 8fl oz) water

Start by making the rice, which you should simply cook according to the instructions on the packet.

Next, make the filling. Heat the oil in a large frying pan over medium heat. Add the onion and saute for 5 minutes until translucent. Add the garlic, mushrooms, chilli flakes, thyme, pepper and salt. Saute for 5 minutes, until the mushrooms are cooked. Add cooked rice and stir, then set aside.

To make the sauce, place all of the sauce ingredients in a saucepan over medium heat and bring to the boil. Immediately reduce the heat, cover and simmer for 5 minutes. Set aside.

Place the cabbage leaves in a large bowl. Fill the bowl with boiling water and cover the bowl with a plate. Allow to sit for 10 minutes to soften the cabbage.

Preheat the oven to 180°C (350°F, Gas Mark 4).

Coat the base of a baking dish with a layer of the sauce.

Take a cabbage leaf and pat dry with paper towel. Place 2-3 tablespoons of the filling mixture at one end of the cabbage leaf. Roll up like a burrito, tucking in the sides. Continue rolling until all leaves are filled.

Place the rolled leaves side by side in the baking dish. Cover with the remaining sauce and place in the oven to bake for 45 minutes.

Beef Empanadas

THINK YOU CAN'T BUT YOU CAN: THESE LITTLE SNACKS ARE EASY TO MAKE AND EVEN EASIER TO EAT

SERVES 24

FILLING

Oil, for frying

800g (1¾ lb) onions, finely chopped

2 garlic cloves, finely chopped

½ red capsicum, finely chopped

600g (1lb 5oz) beef mince

3 tbsps paprika

½ tsp ground cumin

½ tsp ground nutmeg

Salt and pepper, to season

PASTRY

6 cups (750g, 24oz) plain flour

1 tsp salt

300g (10oz) lard, room temperature

1 cup (250ml, 8fl oz) warm water

Heat the oil in a frying pan over a medium-high heat. Add the onion, garlic and capsicum and fry for 5 minutes or until onion is soft. Add the meat and cook for a further 2-3 minutes, stirring, until beef is browned. Now add the paprika, cumin and nutmeg and stir. Reduce the heat to a low simmer and leave to cook for 30 minutes, stirring occasionally. Taste the mixture a few times while it's cooking and season with salt and pepper, if needed.

Place filling in a bowl and cover with plastic wrap. Transfer to the fridge to chill overnight, or for a minimum of 6 hours. Remove from the fridge immediately before use as it needs to be cold.

Next make the pastry. Sift the flour into a large bowl and add salt. Chop the lard into the flour mixture and rub together using your fingertips until a rough crumb forms. Add the water and combine to form a dough. (You can also use an electric mixer for this phase.)

Break the pastry dough into three evenly sized balls. Flour a clean, dry work surface and using a rolling pin begin to roll each ball into a sheet around 3mm (⅛ in) thick. Cut the pastry into discs roughly the same size as a saucer (you can even use a saucer as a guide to cut around). Place the discs on a plate, each one separated by a small piece of baking paper.

Now it's time to remove the filling from the fridge and start creating your empanadas. At this time preheat the oven to 200°C (400°F, Gas Mark 6).

Dampen the edges of each pastry circle, and then fill the centre with a tablespoon of the beef mixture. Fold the circle over and crimp the sides together, using a fork if you like.

Arrange the empanadas on a lined baking tray and transfer to the oven to bake for 15 minutes until golden brown and crispy.

Zucchini and Caraway Quiche

A FLAVOURFUL AND SOPHISTICATED TAKE ON QUICHE LORRAINE THAT IS SUITABLE FOR VEGETARIANS

SERVES 4

SHORTCRUST PASTRY

1¾ cups (215g, 7oz) plain flour, sifted

Pinch of salt

125g (4oz) chilled butter, chopped

1 egg, lightly beaten

1 tbsp iced water

QUICHE FILLING

4 medium zucchinis, julienned

1 tsp salt, divided

1¼ cups (310ml, 10fl oz) milk

1 tsp caraway seeds

½ tsp freshly ground black pepper

3 large eggs, lightly beaten

55g (2oz) plain firm goat's cheese, crumbled

1 yellow capsicum, deseeded and julienned

2 thyme sprigs, cut into 5mm (¼ in) pieces

First, make your pastry. Combine flour and salt in a large bowl. Add butter and rub into flour mixture using fingertips until fine crumbs form. Make a well in the centre of the flour mixture. Combine egg and water in a small bowl, then pour into the well. Using a round-bladed knife, or hands, stir until mixture just forms a dough.

Preheat oven to 220°C (425°F, Gas Mark 7) and grease a springform tart tin.

Turn pastry onto a floured surface and roll into a circle. Press pastry into the tart tin and trim edges. Prick the bottom of the pastry shell with a fork. Line the pastry with baking paper, and fill with dried beans, then place in the oven and blind bake for 20 minutes. Remove beans and paper and return to oven to bake for a further 10 minutes. Remove from oven and cool completely on a wire rack.

Place the zucchini in a large bowl and sprinkle over ½ teaspoon salt. Set aside for 15 minutes to allow the liquid to release. Drain in a colander, squeezing a handful at a time to remove liquid, and then pat dry.

Place the remaining ½ teaspoon salt, milk, caraway seeds, pepper and eggs in a bowl, stirring with a whisk. Sprinkle goat's cheese evenly over the bottom of the prepared crust and then scatter the zucchini and yellow capsicum over the cheese. Gently pour the egg mixture over the top of the vegetables.

Transfer to the oven to bake at 200°C (400°F, Gas Mark 6) for 35 minutes or until egg is set. Let stand 10 minutes before serving.

PASTRY

Ah, pastry: melt-in-your-mouth crumbly, flaky and buttery, pale or dark, sweet or savoury ... how do you know which pastry to use for what and how to avoid the hard, tasteless, chewy varieties?

First of all, one word: frozen. Yes, it's okay to use frozen pastry. It may even be preferable to making your own when it comes to complex pastries such as choux, flaky or filo. These pastries do take time and effort to get right and the results can often not justify the effort. So that really leaves shortcrust as an option for home baking and if you can master a good sweet shortcrust and a good savoury shortcrust you are pretty well sorted for pastry.

Experiment and practise to perfect your shortcrust recipe. A bit of time invested in doing this will create great freedom down the track to be creative with fillings and recipe ideas. Oh, and don't forget that you can freeze your own pastry too. It freezes well, so you'll never be out of stock.

There are a few important considerations to bear in mind when making pastry.

One is temperature. Cold, like Grandma's hands before central heating, is a good way to think of it. There's a scientific reason for this to do with how the flour proteins absorb water, and a practical one too. You need to be able to rub the butter into the flour to create a crumb and you can't do this with butter than melts as you work. Try using your cool fingertips rather than the palm of your hand. Butter coats the flour, minimizing the development of gluten. Too much gluten makes for a tough pastry.

Butter is a big part of the flavour in pastry: use good-quality butter, no exceptions.

Add water slowly and over time you will become a good judge of when enough water has been added. Too much water and too much kneading makes for a tough pastry. Don't overwork the dough. When it comes to rolling, roll in one direction only so the dough doesn't get overstretched and tough.

Take a rest, pastry! Resting allows the gluten to relax, diminishing potential chewiness. Resting the pastry in the fridge is essential as it needs to chill in order to be workable. Don't let it warm up too much when you are ready to roll.

Blind baking is the final unmissable step in a good pastry. This simply means covering the pastry shell with paper and dried beans, and then baking in the oven for 10-15 minutes. This ensures that the base is cooked throughout, so that it doesn't get soggy with the addition of filling.

Remember that even when you have perfected your recipe and technique each batch will be different due to factors such as a different packet of flour or a slight variation in your measurements.

Vanilla Custard

SERVES 8

4 cups (1L, 2pt) milk

⅔ cup (140g, 5oz) sugar

4 tbsps cornflour

2 tsps vanilla extract

4 eggs, beaten

Put the milk, sugar, cornflour and vanilla into a saucepan over a medium heat and bring to a gentle boil.

Immediately remove from the heat and slowly add the beaten eggs, stirring constantly. When all eggs have been added, return the mixture to the stove and cook on a low heat for 5 minutes, or until thick and smooth. Do not allow the custard to boil.

Remove from heat once it simmers. Set aside to cool for a few minutes before serving.

Chocolate Custard

SERVES 8

4 cups (1L, 2pt) milk

⅔ cup (140g, 5oz) sugar

4 tbsps cornflour

⅔ cup (70g, 2½ oz) cocoa powder, sifted

2 tsps vanilla extract

4 eggs, beaten

Whipped cream, to garnish

Mint leaves, to garnish

Put the milk, sugar, cornflour, cocoa powder and vanilla into a saucepan over a medium heat and bring to a gentle boil.

Immediately remove from the heat and slowly add the beaten eggs, stirring constantly. When all eggs have been added, return the mixture to the stove and cook on a low heat for 5 minutes, or until thick and smooth. Do not allow the custard to boil. Remove from heat once it simmers.

Set aside to cool for a few minutes before serving. Place a dollop of whipped cream and a mint leaf on top of each cup to serve.

Portuguese Custard Tarts

SWEET, CREAMY CENTRE OR BUTTERY, FLAKY PASTRY SHELLS? TAKE
YOUR PICK, BOTH ELEMENTS OF THIS CLASSIC TREAT ARE TO DIE FOR

SERVES 12

2 egg yolks

1 whole egg

½ cup (110g, 4oz)
caster sugar

1½ tbsps cornflour

1¼ cups (310ml, 10fl
oz) milk

1 cup (250ml, 8fl oz)
thickened cream

1½ tsps vanilla
extract

1 tbsp caster sugar

2 tsps ground
cinnamon

2 sheets frozen puff
pastry, partially thawed

Preheat oven to 210°C (410°F, Gas Mark 6). Grease a 12-hole muffin tin.

Whisk egg yolks, whole egg, sugar and cornflour in a medium saucepan until well combined. Slowly add the milk and then the cream, stirring to combine.

Turn heat on to low and cook the custard, stirring constantly with the whisk until it comes to a simmer and begins to thicken. Remove from heat and stir in the vanilla. Transfer custard to a heatproof bowl and cover with plastic wrap. Place in the fridge for 1 hour.

Combine sugar and cinnamon and sprinkle half of the mixture over one of the pastry sheets. Cover with the other pastry sheet and then sprinkle with remaining cinnamon sugar. Press the two sheets together using a rolling pin. Firmly roll the two sheets of pastry together into a log. Using a sharp knife, cut the pastry log into 12 even portions.

Place a pastry portion on a floured bench top. Flatten slightly then roll into a 10cm (4in) circle. Gently press the pastry round into a muffin tin hole. Repeat with the remaining pastry portions.

Spoon the cooled custard evenly into the pastry cases. Bake in preheated oven for 30 minutes or until the pastry is crisp and the custard golden on top.

Remove from oven and stand the tarts in the tin for 5 minutes before transferring to a wire rack to cool completely. Serve at room temperature.

Swedish Pancake Cake with Chocolate Sauce and Berries

A DECADENT DELICIOUS PLATE TO SHARE WITH FRIENDS —
MAKE SURE THERE'S A PIECE LEFT FOR YOU!

SERVES 6

PANCAKES

1⅔ cups (205g, 7oz) buckwheat flour

3 large eggs (or 4 medium)

2 cups (500ml, 1pt) milk

1 cup (250ml, 8fl oz) water

Pinch sea salt

1 tbsp butter, plus extra for frying

CHOCOLATE SAUCE

300g (10oz) good-quality dark chocolate, chopped

1¼ cups (300ml, 10fl oz) thin cream

CREAM

2 cups (500ml, 1pt) thick cream, chilled

Raspberries and chopped pistachio nuts, to serve

To make the batter, place all the pancake ingredients into a large mixing bowl and whisk vigorously until you have a smooth, lump-free batter. Cover and place in the fridge to chill for 20 minutes. Remove the batter from the fridge and whisk to re-incorporate the ingredients.

Heat a medium-sized frying pan over medium-high heat. When the pan is hot, add 1 teaspoon of butter and about ⅓ cup (75ml, 2½ fl oz) of batter. Tilt the pan until the batter is thinly and evenly distributed. Fry until bubbles appear in the batter; the pancake should be golden and easily flipped with a spatula. Repeat until the batter has been used up (you should have around 15 pancakes) and place each one on baking paper to cool. To stop the pancakes sticking together layer each one on fresh baking paper.

Next make the sauce. Place the chocolate in a bowl. Place cream in a pan over medium heat and bring to just below boiling point. Pour the cream over the chocolate, then stir until smooth.

Pour the cold cream into a large chilled bowl. Use an electric hand mixer or a whisk to whip it until soft peaks form. Set aside.

Put the first cooled pancake on a cake stand or serving platter. Add a layer of cream, then chocolate sauce. Repeat with the remaining pancakes until all have been used up, finishing with a generous layer of cream and sauce. Finish off with fresh berries and pistachio nuts.

Chocolate Salami

A SECRET WEAPON IN YOUR ENTERTAINING ARSENAL, THIS CHOCOLATE SALAMI IS JUST SO EASY TO MAKE

SERVES 6

200g (7oz) dark chocolate (60% cacao or more)

110g (4oz) butter

2 egg yolks

1 tbsp sugar

1 tbsp cocoa powder

Pinch of salt

2 tbsps dark rum

200g (7oz) cookies, broken into pieces

Icing sugar, for rolling

Place the chocolate and butter in a medium-sized saucepan over a low heat and cook for 2-3 minutes to allow the butter and chocolate to melt. Stir to combine, then add the egg yolks. Stir constantly for 1 minute until all the ingredients are well combined.

Add the sugar, cocoa powder, salt and rum and stir well. Finally add the broken cookies and stir again. Set aside to cool slightly so that you can handle the mixture.

Spoon the mixture in a line in the centre of a piece of baking paper. Roll the paper around the mixture to form a log shape. Wrap the log in plastic wrap and transfer to the fridge for 1 hour or until 30 minutes before you are ready to serve.

Remove from the fridge. Shake the icing sugar onto a clean, dry work surface. Unwrap the log from its plastic and paper packaging and roll it gently in the icing sugar. Slice into rounds using a sharp knife.

Rum and Raisin Truffles

MAKES 20

¼ cup (40g, 1½ oz) raisins, chopped

¼ cup (60ml, 2fl oz) rum

½ cup (125ml, 4fl oz) heavy cream

1½ tbsps unsalted butter

200g (7oz) dark chocolate (at least 70% cacao), broken into pieces

2 tbsps cocoa powder, plus extra for rolling

1 tsp vanilla extract

Soak the raisins in rum for 1 hour.

Bring the cream to a simmer in a medium saucepan over a low heat. Add the butter and stir until melted. Then add the chopped chocolate, and stir until just melting. Remove from the heat to melt completely. Mix in the cocoa powder and vanilla extract and stir until smooth. Finally, stir in the raisin-rum mixture.

Place in a covered bowl and transfer to the fridge. Chill for 2 hours until firm.

Dust the cocoa onto a clean, dry work surface. Using your hands, roll the chocolate mixture into balls, then roll each ball through the cocoa until coated. Store in a lined airtight container in the fridge.

Easy Chocolate Truffles

MAKES 15

170g (6oz) dark chocolate (at least 70% cacao), broken into pieces

⅓ cup (80ml, 3fl oz) heavy cream

1 tsp vanilla extract

½ cup (40g, 1½ oz) desiccated coconut

Place the chocolate in the microwave on high for 30 seconds. Stir and repeat until chocolate has melted completely.

Place the cream in a small saucepan over medium heat. When just simmering, pour over the melted chocolate. Add the vanilla and stir until well combined.

Place in a covered bowl and transfer to the fridge. Chill for 2 hours until firm.

Scatter the coconut onto a clean, dry work surface. Using your hands, roll the chocolate mixture into balls, then roll each ball through the coconut flakes until coated. Store in a lined airtight container in the fridge.

CHOCOLATE TRUFFLES

Get creative and coat your truffles in a variety of toppings to surprise and inspire your guests. Add colour and variety to this classic dessert with coatings such as shredded coconut, cocoa powder, chopped nuts, candied peel, hundreds and thousands and melted white chocolate drizzled in various patterns. Always make sure you lay baking paper down on the tray before placing the truffles on top to set – you don't want your beautiful creations to stick!

Lemon Meringue Pie

TRADITIONAL DESSERTS DON'T GET MORE TANGY, CREAMY AND CRUNCHY THAN THIS GOOD OLD-FASHIONED LEMON MERINGUE PIE

SERVES 10

PASTRY

1¾ cups (215g, 7oz) plain flour

1 tbsp icing sugar

140g (5oz) butter, chilled and coarsely chopped

1 egg yolk

2 tbsps iced water

FILLING

½ cup (75g, 3oz) cornflour

1½ cups (330g, 12oz) caster sugar

½ cup (125ml, 4fl oz) lemon juice

1¼ cups (310ml, 10fl oz) water

2 tsps lemon rind, finely grated

80g (3oz) butter, coarsely chopped

3 eggs, separated

Rub flour, icing sugar and butter together with fingertips until crumbly. Add egg yolk and iced water. Mix until ingredients come together. Knead dough on floured surface until smooth. Form into a ball and wrap in plastic wrap. Refrigerate for 30 minutes.

Grease a 24cm (9½ in) springform fluted flan tin. Roll pastry large enough to line the tin. Using a rolling pin, fold pastry into the tin. Press gently into the base and sides and trim edges with a sharp knife. Cover with plastic wrap and refrigerate for 30 minutes.

Preheat the oven to 200°C (390°F, Gas Mark 6). Blind bake for 15 minutes, then remove the paper and weights from the pastry case. Bake for a further 10 minutes until golden. Remove and set aside to cool.

Combine cornflour and 1 cup (220g, 8oz) of the caster sugar in a medium saucepan. Gradually stir in lemon juice and water and stir until smooth. Cook over a high heat until mixture boils and then thickens. Reduce heat and simmer, stirring, for 1 minute. Remove from heat. Stir in rind and butter and, quickly, stir in egg yolks. Set aside to cool for 10 minutes.

Spoon the filling into the pastry case and spread evenly across the base. Cover and refrigerate for 2 hours.

Preheat oven to 220°C (430°F, Gas Mark 7).

Beat the egg whites with an electric mixer until soft peaks form. Slowly add remaining sugar, beating until sugar dissolves and glossy, firm peaks form.

Spread meringue mixture on top of the lemon filling. Bake for 20 minutes or until meringue is golden brown.

Dinner Party

OYSTERS

Love 'em or hate 'em, oysters rarely elicit a shrug of the shoulders. Let's assume for the sake of your dinner party that you've checked out your guests' feelings on the matter and have invited only those with the finest of tastes – oyster lovers, of course.

Now that you've set the bar, the pressure is on to deliver. First of all, and absolutely most important, is to pick good oysters. One way is to know the person you are buying from – let's assume a market stall trader – that's a great way to be sure of quality. If you don't have that luxury, then look out for plump, juicy or wet-looking oysters that have a sheen to them. You should be able to smell the fresh sea smell. A fishy smell is a definite no-no and a sign that your oysters are on their way out. If you want to ask a question of your vendor, ask when the oysters were harvested and don't buy if they've been out of the water for longer than a week.

KNOW YOUR OYSTERS

You'll want to impress your dinner guests with your knowledge of what you are serving. 'Sure,' you say, 'there are over a hundred varieties of oysters but did you know that all of these derive from just five species?' Interesting fact. And the names of these five: Pacific oysters, Kumamoto oysters, European flat oysters, Atlantic oysters and Olympia oysters.

Pacific oysters are small and sweet and the world's most cultivated oysters. Atlantic oysters are farmed over a huge area so flavour can vary but generally speaking they are more salty than the Pacific variety. Less common, Kumamotos are small, almost nutty oysters characterised by their deep shell. European flats have a flatter shell, a meaty flesh, and a sharp, mineral taste, and Olympias are tiny, sweet and a little bit metallic to the taste.

THE CLASSICS

Naked – plain, raw, unadulterated oysters. Many oyster lovers will only eat them this way. To make them look a bit special serve on a chilled platter of rock salt with lemon wedges. **Oysters Kilpatrick** – this is the old-school dish of the oyster world, topped with bacon, Worcestershire sauce and parsley and served with lemon wedges. **Rockefeller** – oysters topped with a green sauce made from butter, spinach, parsley and various other ingredients according to the particular recipe. **Mignonette** – an oyster-fave condiment usually made with minced shallots, cracked pepper and vinegar.

Cooking opens the door to a whole new world of recipe ideas. Some of the best include grilling oysters, pan-frying them with burnt butter, roasting them or, of course, creating a delicious chowder.

Baked Mussels with Cheese

A SIMPLE, DOABLE RECIPE FOR MUSSELS THAT EVERYBODY CAN ENJOY

SERVES 20

20 large green mussels

¼ cup (60ml, 2fl oz) water

60g (2oz) butter

3 garlic cloves, finely chopped

½ cup (60g, 2oz) breadcrumbs

3 tbsps parsley, chopped

½ cup (60g, 2oz) Cheddar cheese, grated

¼ cup (30g, 1oz) Parmesan cheese, grated

Salt and pepper, to taste

1 lemon, wedged

Place the mussels and water in a large saucepan or stockpot over a medium heat. Bring to the boil and then reduce the heat, and cook for a further 4-6 minutes or until the mussels open. As each one opens scoop it out with a slotted spoon and set aside to cool so you can handle them. When cool, remove the top shell and place face up on a baking tray.

Place the butter in a frying pan over a medium heat and when melted add the garlic. Fry for a few minutes, stirring to ensure that it doesn't burn. Add the breadcrumbs and stir for 3-4 minutes until they crisp up, then add the parsley and stir for a further minute. Remove from the heat.

Turn on the griller and set to 180°C (350°F, Gas Mark 4).

Place a teaspoon of breadcrumb mixture on top of each mussel, and then finish with a teaspoon of Cheddar and Parmesan.

Place mussels under the griller for 8-10 minutes or until the cheese has melted and turned golden brown in colour.

Season with salt and pepper and serve with a squeeze of lemon.

Prawn Shooters

MAKE THIS SPICY SHOOTER THE NIGHT BEFORE FOR SOME EXTRA PUNCH

SERVES 8

1 tsp vegetable oil

Small piece galangal (or ginger), sliced

2 garlic cloves, chopped

5 kaffir lime leaves, torn

1 stalk lemongrass, bashed and chopped

⅓ cup (100ml, 3½ fl oz) rice wine vinegar

450g (1lb) tomatoes, chopped

½ cucumber, peeled, deseeded and chopped

1 green bird's-eye chilli, chopped

½ red capsicum, chopped

½ shallot, chopped

1 tsp fish sauce

1 tsp Sriracha sauce

Lime juice, to taste

Pinch of sugar

8 cooked king prawns, deveined, peeled, tails intact

Sliced cucumber and mint, to garnish

Heat the oil in a small saucepan over a medium heat. Add the galangal, garlic, kaffir lime leaves and lemongrass and cook, stirring, for 2 minutes until soft and fragrant. Add the rice wine vinegar and bring the mixture to a gentle simmer. Remove from the heat and set aside to cool slightly.

Place the mixture in a food processor along with the tomatoes, cucumber, chilli, capsicum and shallot.

Blitz until the desired consistency is reached – it's good to have a smooth base to the mixture with some chunky pieces remaining to add texture.

Pour the mixture into a bowl or jug. Add the remaining ingredients apart from the prawns and garnish and stir to combine. Cover and transfer to the fridge to chill overnight or for a minimum of 2 hours.

When ready to serve, pour into individual shot glasses. Place a prawn in each glass along with the garnishes.

MICRO GREENS

Micro greens are tiny edible leaves that are less than 14 days old! They differ from sprouts in that they are grown in soil, not water. Used both as garnishes and main ingredients, micro greens add exquisite colour and texture to your meals and have a multitude of subtle flavours. Commonly used micro greens include rocket, beet greens, kale, onions, radish greens, watercress and herbs.

Avocado & Salmon Verrines

SERVES 4

2 ripe avocados, peeled and chopped

80g (3oz) creme fraiche

150g (5oz) Boursin garlic and fine herbs cheese

1 tbsp lemon juice

Pinch salt and pepper

2 tsps fresh dill, chopped, plus sprigs for garnish

240g (8oz) smoked salmon

Put the avocado and creme fraiche in the bowl of a food processor or high-speed blender. Quickly pulse to break down, then add the Boursin, lemon juice, salt, pepper and fresh dill, and blend until smooth.

Slice the smoked salmon into small pieces, and set aside.

To serve, fill four shot glasses with a spoonful of avocado mousse and top with salmon pieces and a garnish of fresh dill.

Quinoa Salad

SERVES 8

DRESSING

3 tbsps lime juice

1 tbsp white wine vinegar

1 tbsp honey

2 tsps ground cumin

1 tsp sea salt

½ tsp ground black pepper

6-8 tbsps olive oil

SALAD

1 large bunch radishes, thinly sliced

3 spring onions, thinly sliced

¼ cup (10g, ¼ oz) fresh dill, chopped

½ cup (100g, 3oz) quinoa, cooked

To make the dressing, combine all the ingredients in a small bowl or jar with a sealable lid and whisk or shake to combine. Season to taste with salt and pepper.

Combine the radishes, spring onions and dill in a large bowl and gently toss to mix. Add the quinoa. Add the dressing and toss to combine.

Spicy Radicchio Wraps with Peanut Sauce

A CRUNCHY FRESH STARTER PERFECT FOR A SUMMER'S EVENING WITH FRIENDS

SERVES 4

2 boneless, skinless chicken breasts, cooked

2 tsps salt

PEANUT SAUCE

4 tbsps creamy peanut butter

3 tbsps soy sauce

2 tbsps water

½ tsp garlic powder

2 tsps brown sugar

1 tsp Sriracha sauce

⅛ tsp sesame oil

¼ cup (30g, 1oz) roasted peanuts, roughly chopped

FILLING

1 red capsicum, thinly sliced

2 carrots, peeled and thinly sliced

2-3 leaves butter lettuce

1 head radicchio, leaves separated

Fresh coriander and dill, to garnish

First poach the chicken. Place the chicken breasts in a large saucepan and cover with water. Season with salt. Bring to the boil over a high heat and then immediately reduce to a simmer. Simmer the chicken for 5 minutes, removing any scum that surfaces at the top of the water. Remove chicken from the water and set aside to rest for 10 minutes before slicing.

Next make the sauce. Combine all the ingredients in a small bowl or blender and whisk or blend to combine all the ingredients. Taste and adjust seasonings as required.

Thinly slice the chicken and place in a large mixing bowl. Add the capsicum, carrots and butter lettuce and toss to combine.

Spoon the chicken and capsicum mixture into the radicchio leaves, then top with peanut sauce and chopped herbs.

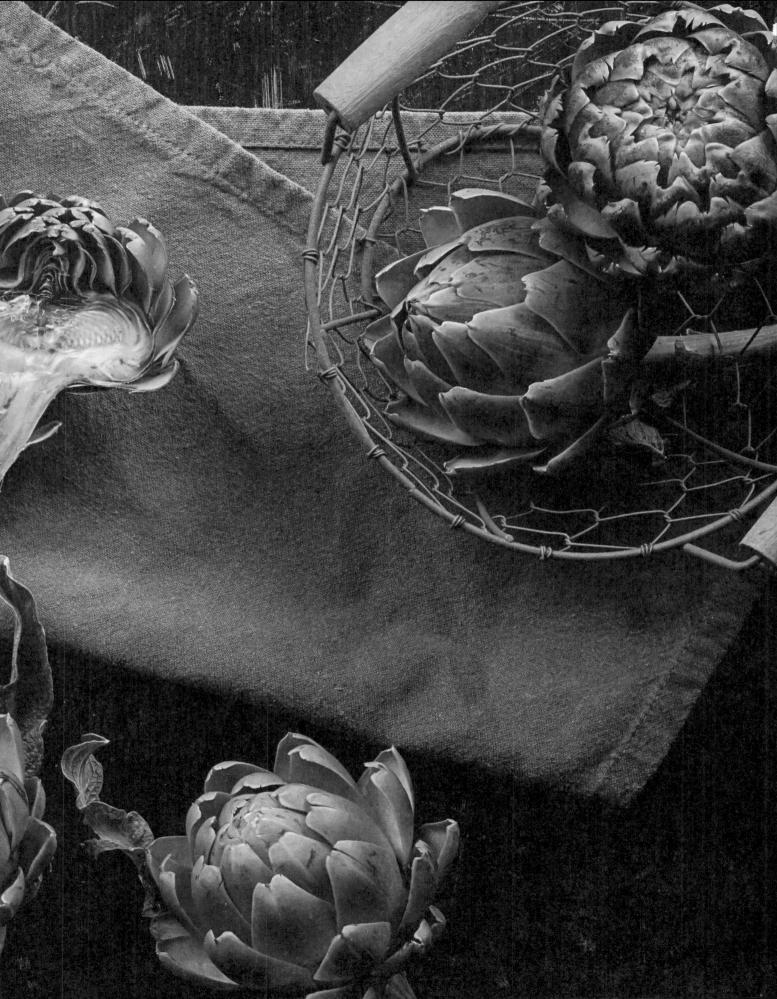

Spinach and Artichoke Dip

SERVES 4

2 tbsps olive oil

1 garlic clove, finely chopped

500g (1lb 2oz) baby spinach leaves, finely chopped

1 x 400g (14oz) jar artichoke hearts, drained and chopped

¼ cup (40g, 1½ oz) green olives, finely chopped

Sea salt and black pepper

225g (8oz, ½ lb) cream cheese, cut into cubes

120g (4oz) fresh mozzarella, torn or shredded

½ cup (125g, 4oz) Greek yoghurt

¼ cup (30g, 1oz) Parmesan cheese, finely grated

Heat olive oil in a medium saucepan over medium heat. Add garlic and cook, stirring, for about 30 seconds.

Add the spinach to the pan one handful at a time, letting each batch wilt before adding the next. Continue to cook, stirring frequently, until most of the liquid from the spinach has evaporated. Add artichokes and olives and season with salt and pepper. Cook for a few minutes.

Reduce heat to low, then add cream cheese and mozzarella. Stir until all the cheese has melted, then stir in yoghurt and Parmesan, and season with more salt and pepper if needed. Let the dip cool and serve as needed.

Grilled Chicken Pasta

SERVES 4

600g chicken breasts, cut into thick slices

⅓ cup (80ml, 3fl oz) olive oil, plus more for drizzling

⅓ cup (80ml, 3fl oz) lemon juice, plus more for drizzling

200g (7oz) baby spinach leaves, finely chopped

2 tsps lemon zest

¼ cup (10g, ¼ oz) parsley, finely chopped

½ tsp salt

½ tsp black pepper

3 medium zucchinis, sliced into batons

300g (10oz) fettucini, cooked until al dente

Place chicken pieces in a large container with a sealable lid. Whisk together olive oil, lemon juice, spinach, lemon zest, parsley, salt and pepper. Pour half the mixture over the chicken, making sure to coat each piece. Cover and marinate for 30 minutes at room temperature. Toss zucchini slices in remaining marinade.

Grill zucchini slices over medium heat for 6 minutes, flipping once, until tender. Grill chicken slices over high heat for 10 minutes, turning once.

Mix the chicken and zucchini through the fettucini and serve.

Gourmet Fish and Chips with Artichoke and Potato Rounds

SPRUCE UP AN OLD FAVE — AND YOU'LL HAVE A WINNER OF A DISH FOR A QUICK AND TASTY SUPPER WITH FRIENDS

SERVES 4

2 large potatoes (a starchy variety is best for this)

1 tbsp olive oil

1 tbsp butter, melted

½ tsp sea salt

1 x 400g (14oz) jar artichoke hearts, drained and chopped

FISH

Olive oil for frying

50g (2oz) butter

1 garlic clove, crushed

1 lemon, zested

1½ tbsps lemon juice

4 snapper fillets

Salt and pepper

1 tbsp cornflour

1 tbsp olive oil, for frying

2 tbsps butter, for frying

½ cup (20g, ¾ oz) parsley, finely chopped

First, get the potatoes cooking. Preheat the oven to 230°C (450°F, Gas Mark 8). Scrub the potatoes, leaving them unpeeled, and cut into thick rounds. Combine olive oil and melted butter in a small bowl. Arrange the potato slices, with a bit of space between them, in rows on a baking sheet. Lightly brush the potatoes with the oil mixture. Transfer to the oven to bake for 20 minutes, or until they are golden and crisp, turning once during cooking. Transfer the potatoes to paper towel to drain and sprinkle with the salt. Place the artichoke pieces into the tray with the potato and cover with foil to keep warm if needed.

Heat the butter over a low heat and add the garlic. Cook for 2-3 minutes until fragrant but not brown. Add lemon zest and juice. Keep warm.

Season the fish with salt and pepper, then dust with cornflour. Shake off the excess.

Heat the oil and butter in a large frying pan over a medium-high heat. When the butter foams, place fish fillets in the pan (fit as many as you can cook comfortably, don't cram them in). Cook for around 4 minutes until the bottom is golden brown. Flip and cook on the other side for 1 minute. Remove and keep warm until serving.

Serve fish on top of potato rounds and artichoke hearts, and pour over the lemon sauce from the pan.

Salmon with Asparagus and Lemon Tarragon Cream Sauce

A DELICATE CREAM SAUCE TRANSFORMS THIS SIMPLE DISH INTO AN ELEGANT AND DELICIOUS SUPPER

SERVES 4

4 salmon fillets

Salt and pepper

2 tbsps olive oil

2 bunches of asparagus, trimmed

LEMON TARRAGON CREAM SAUCE

1 tbsp butter or olive oil

2 garlic cloves

1 cup (250ml, 8fl oz) cream

1 tsp lemon zest

2 tbsps chopped fresh tarragon

2 tbsps fresh lemon juice

Salt and pepper

Remove salmon fillets from the fridge around 15 minutes before cooking, allowing time for them to come to room temperature. Pat salmon fillets dry with a paper towel then season both sides with salt and pepper.

Heat a frying pan over a medium-high heat until very hot. Add a splash of olive oil, then add the salmon fillets skin side down. Cook uninterrupted for 4-8 minutes depending on the thickness of your salmon. The salmon is ready to turn when the deep orange colour has turned to a lighter pink colour about three-quarters of the way up the side of the fish. Turn the fish over and cook for 2-3 minutes on the other side.

While the salmon is cooking, blanch the asparagus for 2-3 minutes in boiling water until bright green and tender.

To make the sauce, place the butter or oil and the garlic in a small saucepan over a medium heat. Allow to cook gently for 2 minutes, then add the cream, lemon zest and chopped tarragon. Cook for a further 2-3 minutes or until the desired thickness is reached. Add lemon juice, salt and pepper and stir to combine.

Serve salmon and asparagus drizzled with the sauce.

Halibut with Soy-Ginger Sauce

THESE TENDER FISH FILLETS ARE DELICIOUS SERVED WITH A SIMPLE BUT FLAVOURFUL SAUCE

SERVES 6

¼ cup (60ml, 2fl oz) plus 2 tbsps soy sauce

3 tbsps rice wine vinegar

2 tbsps mirin

2 tbsps grapeseed oil

2 tsps Asian sesame oil

¼ cup (15g, ½ oz) fresh ginger, peeled and finely julienned

8 Asian shallots, peeled and quartered

4 thick halibut fillets, skinned (substitute snapper or cod)

TOMATO SALSA

4 ripe tomatoes, finely chopped

2 spring onions, finely sliced

Handful of basil leaves, finely chopped

To make the sauce, combine the soy sauce, rice wine vinegar, mirin, grapeseed and sesame oils and ginger in a small bowl.

Place the fish fillets in a large shallow dish and brush with half of the sauce. Cover and refrigerate for 30 minutes.

Preheat the oven to 230°C (450°F, Gas Mark 8). Place the shallots in the bottom of a large, ovenproof dish and put the fish fillets on top. Transfer to the oven to bake for 15 minutes, or until lightly coloured and just cooked through.

Make the simple salsa by combining the tomato, spring onion and basil in a bowl.

Serve the fish fillets with the remaining soy-ginger sauce and tomato salsa.

PERFECT PULLED PORK

Traditionally the kind of dish you'd cook for hours and hours in a large charcoal pit, pulled pork has hit the mainstream in recent years, dispensing with the need for a charcoal pit – although hours and hours are still recommended to get this dish right.

The first consideration to make is the cut of meat. Pork shoulder is an excellent choice. Bone-in is best as this ensures the meat remains tender. Bone-out can cause meat to dry, but if you are careful with the recipe you choose this cut should work well too.

To do this thing properly, you'll want to apply a salt rub to the meat. Remove and discard the skin before you do this, then simply mix sea salt, sugar and paprika together in a bag and then rub, rub, rub with your fingers into the flesh of the pork. You can explore variations and additions to this mix if you like. Cover and place in the fridge overnight. When you remove the meat to prepare for cooking, be sure to rinse thoroughly or your final dish will be salty, and not in a good way.

A super-low oven temperature is what's required for cooking – say, 140°C (285°F, Gas Mark 1). To prepare your joint for the oven place it on the wire rack of a roasting tin. Pour water into the bottom of the tin and then wrap the whole kit and caboodle tightly in aluminium foil. If this sounds too complicated, you could just use a Dutch oven. Cook for 4 hours minimum and longer as needed for the pork to form a dark glue on the outside and the meat to collapse when a fork is inserted into it.

Next, you need to shred your pork. An easy way to do this is simply to use two forks, pulling the meat out from the centre. Don't overdo it. It's nice for dinners to have some big chunks of meat too.

Every good pulled pork needs a good sauce. A simple BBQ sauce is a great option. Smoky flavour is a great companion to pulled pork, so anything with chipotle is sure to be a winner. Other popular choices are mustard sauce, vinegar sauce, home-made ketchup or sweet chilli sauce.

Don't forget to think accessories. You can't go past a coleslaw and you'll be amazed at the variety of recipes out there transforming the humble slaw into a flavour sensation. See page 182 for some ideas. Breads are great for rounding out the meal, and depending on your recipe, you could consider Mexican-style tortillas or US-style hamburgers, or for a contemporary twist on the hamburger a brioche bun works well.

And finally, pulled pork is the prince of leftovers: think pulled pork wraps, sandwiches, rice paper rolls. You're all set for the week!

Classic BBQ Sauce

SERVES 3 (1½ CUPS)

1½ cups (375ml, 13fl oz) tomato sauce

½ cup (80g, 3oz) packed dark brown sugar

2 garlic cloves, minced

3 tbsps cider vinegar

3 tbsps Worcestershire sauce

1 tbsp molasses

½ tsp Tabasco (or other hot sauce)

1 tsp paprika

¾ tsp pepper

½ cup (125ml, 4fl oz) water

Place all ingredients in a small saucepan over medium heat.

Bring to a boil, stirring until well combined.

Reduce heat to low and cook, uncovered, on a gentle simmer for 30 minutes until the sauce has thickened and flavour developed.

Remove from heat and set aside to cool.

Asian Slaw

SERVES 4

2 carrots

¼ head small red cabbage

1 small cucumber, chopped

1 tbsp white sesame seeds

DRESSING

2 tbsps lime juice

2 tbsps sesame oil

2 tbsps soy sauce

1½ tbsps rice wine vinegar

1 tbsp brown sugar

1 red chilli, deseeded and coarsely chopped

1 garlic clove, finely chopped

Small piece fresh ginger, finely grated

Finely julienne the carrots and red cabbage using a mandolin or very sharp knife. Combine all the slaw ingredients together in a bowl.

Combine all the dressing ingredients in a bowl or jar with a tight-fitting lid. Whisk or shake to combine.

Pour dressing over the slaw and toss well to coat.

COLESLAW

Coleslaw is so varied these days, it makes you wonder what it's actually supposed to be. Answer: cabbage salad. With that in mind, so long as you have a healthy amount of cabbage in the recipe you can go for your life with the other ingredients. Popular options include, of course, the mighty carrot, onion (controversial), apples and nuts. Another key factor in your slaw is your choice of dressing. Traditionally, mayonnaise has been used. Nowadays a yoghurt-based dressing or even a vinegar or citrus-based dressing is a perfectly acceptable alternative. Kings of the slaws these days are Mexican and Asian slaws that add a bit of spice and saltiness to the traditional recipes.

Honey-Roasted Red Cabbage

AN EXCELLENT CHOICE FOR A SIDE DISH, FULL OF FLAVOUR, COLOUR AND TEXTURE

SERVES 4

1 medium red cabbage, washed

½ cup (180g, 6 oz) honey

Salt and ground pepper

Olive oil

Balsamic vinegar

2 tbsps fresh thyme leaves

Preheat oven to 200°C (400°F, Gas Mark 6).

Slice the cabbage and place it into a large roasting dish.

Drizzle over the honey and season generously with the salt and pepper.

Splash over a good slug or two of olive oil and 2-3 tablespoons of water and toss to coat the cabbage thoroughly.

Cover with aluminum foil and roast in the oven for about 20-25 minutes, then remove the aluminum and toss the cabbage again.

Roast for another 15 to 20 minutes and again mix halfway, until the cabbage is cooked through – it should become crispy on the edges.

Splash a generous amount of balsamic vinegar over the cabbage. Add the fresh thyme leaves, mix gently and roast for another 15 minutes until the vinegar has evaporated.

Transfer to a serving plate and serve immediately. Garnish with a few sprigs of thyme.

Potato Tarte Tatin

SIMPLICITY, FLAVOUR AND ALL CLASS, THIS FRENCH DISH WILL IMPRESS AND DELIGHT YOUR DINNER GUESTS

SERVES 4

5 medium potatoes, peeled and sliced into thick rounds

1 small onion, sliced

¼ cup (60ml, 2fl oz) olive oil

Sea salt and ground black pepper

⅓ cup (50g, 2oz) brown sugar

1 tbsp white wine vinegar

1½ tsps rosemary, chopped

1½ tsps fresh thyme, chopped

120g (4oz) fresh goat's cheese (optional)

1-2 sheets frozen puff pastry, thawed

Preheat oven to 200°C (400°F, Gas Mark 6). Lightly grease a 23cm x 4 cm (9 x 1½ in) pie dish.

In a bowl, add the sliced potato and onion and sprinkle over olive oil and salt and pepper. Place the slices on a large baking tray in a single layer. Roast until just browned around the edges and slightly softened for 30-35 minutes. Let cool.

In a small saucepan, gently heat the sugar and 2 tablespoons of water for at least 5 minutes until is the sugar is dissolved. Remove from heat and stir through the vinegar and a pinch of salt. Immediately pour the caramel into the pie dish. Tilt the dish around so that the caramel coats the bottom as evenly as you can get it. Sprinkle the rosemary and thyme over the top.

Arrange the potatoes in a single layer on top of the caramel, using any smaller slices to fill in gaps. Spread the onion rings and crumble the goat's cheese over the top.

Place a sheet of puff pastry over the top of the dish ensuring it's completely covered and tuck the edges into the dish. Prick the pastry all over with a fork.

Bake in the lower third of the oven for 20 minutes, then reduce the temperature to 180°C (350°F, Gas Mark 4) and bake further for 15 mins or until the crust is golden brown.

Let your tart cool for at least 5 minutes before very carefully turning upside down onto a large plate.

Balsamic Green Beans and Mushrooms

AN ORIGINAL SIDE DISH WITH AN INTERESTING FLAVOUR OF ITS OWN CAN BE HARD TO FIND — HERE'S ONE

SERVES 4

460g (1lb) green beans, trimmed

1 tsp light olive oil

8 medium button mushrooms, thickly sliced

4 medium oyster mushrooms, thickly sliced

Flaked sea salt and ground black pepper

¼ cup (60ml, 2fl oz) balsamic vinegar

Bring a pot of water to the boil and add a handful of salt. Stir, then add the beans. Boil for 5 minutes or less until softened. Strain.

While the water is coming to a boil, place a medium frying pan over medium heat. Add the olive oil to the pan. When hot, add the mushrooms. Sprinkle with a pinch of flaked salt and freshly ground black pepper then stir. Saute for about 6-8 minutes, stirring occasionally, until mushrooms have begun to caramelise.

Add the strained green beans to the pan and stir. Add the balsamic vinegar to deglaze the pan, stirring to scrape up any bits stuck to the bottom. Allow the vinegar to almost completely evaporate, leaving a shiny glaze all over the beans and mushrooms.

Remove from heat and adjust taste with seasoning as needed.

GRANITA

Granita is basically sorbet, but made by hand rather than with a machine, so it's all nice and crunchy. It can be served as a dessert, a drink or as a palate cleanser between courses.

It has a noble and romantic past. Granita is from Sicily, where Arab influences are strong. The Arabs are reported to have brought to Sicily their sherbet, an icy drink flavoured with fruit or with that most Arabian of ingredients, rose water. It is said that snow was harvested from the slopes of Mount Etna and other nearby mountains by snow dealers who stored it in grottos. This snow then became the integral part of the thirst-quenching drink.

Palermo, the capital of Sicily, is still famed for its granita – coffee and almond varieties are popular there and across Italy. They are often served in a glass for breakfast along with a brioche. Toasted almond and strawberry are popular flavours, as well as the more experimental flavours such as pomegranate, pistachio or chocolate. The adventurous-minded could even consider savoury granita – cucumber, tomato, basil? Lemon granita is a staple version, but the golden rule of granita in Italy as it should be all over the world is keep it seasonal – granita these days is a fruit drink so the best way to give it a great flavour is to use whatever fruit is in season.

HOW TO MAKE A CLASSIC LEMON GRANITA

First make a syrup by combining 2 cups (500ml, 1pt) of water and ¾ cup (165g, 6oz) sugar in a small saucepan over a low heat. Stir until the sugar is dissolved then remove from the heat.

Stir in the zest of two lemons and allow the syrup to cool. When cool, strain and discard the lemon zest.

Juice the lemons (use enough to make ½ cup, 125ml, 4fl oz) and stir this juice into the syrup. Add a cup (250ml, 8fl oz) of water and stir to combine.

Pour the mixture into a shallow tray and put it in the freezer. Take it out every 30 minutes and stir with a fork to break up the ice crystals. Keep doing this for 3 hours, or longer for a firmer granita.

You can use an ice-cream maker too. This will give a slushier but still yummy result.

Serve this granita any time of day. It's great for morning tea on a hot summer's day.

HOW TO MAKE A CLASSIC COFFEE GRANITA

Follow the steps above, but substitute the seeds of a vanilla pod for the lemon rind and a couple of shots of espresso for the lemon juice.

Serve in glasses for dessert with whipped cream and amaretti.

Tiramisu

WHY WOULD ANYONE GO TO ITALY WHEN THEY CAN COME
TO YOUR PLACE FOR THIS?

SERVES 8

2 large eggs

⅓ cup (70g, 2½ oz) caster sugar

2½ cups (550ml, 20fl oz) espresso or very strong black coffee, cooled

460g (1lb) mascarpone cheese

400g (14oz) lady finger biscuits – crisp, not sponge

150g (5oz) plain dark chocolate, grated

2½ tsps unsweetened cocoa powder

Separate the eggs. In a medium bowl, whisk the egg yolks and sugar together until the mixture is thick, pale yellow, and forms a ribbon when the whisk is lifted out of the bowl, about 1 minute. Add ¼ cup (60ml, 2fl oz) coffee and the mascarpone and whisk until the mixture is smooth.

In a separate bowl, whisk the egg whites until soft peaks form when you lift the whisk out of the bowl. Gently fold the egg white into the mascarpone mixture.

Dip the biscuits, one at a time, into the remaining coffee; let them soak just long enough to become damp but not soggy.

Place one or two biscuits into the bottom of each glass or serving bowl – enough to form a layer. Break the biscuits up if you need to. Sprinkle over about ½ teaspoon of the grated chocolate and layer over that around 2cm (1in) of the mascarpone mixture. Repeat until you get to the top of the glass or bowl then cover with plastic wrap and leave in the fridge until the mascarpone mixture is set, 8-10 hours or overnight.

When you are ready to serve, place the cocoa powder in a small sieve and dust over the top of the tiramisu.

Coffee Mousse with Orange Sauce

THIS FRAGRANT DESSERT IS A BRIGHT CITRUS TWIST ON
AN OLD CLASSIC

SERVES 4

¾ cup (200ml, 7fl oz) cream

3 tbsps espresso coffee

3 eggs

½ cup (110g, 4oz) caster sugar

Cooking salt

30g (1oz) candied orange peel or slices of orange and mint leaves, to garnish

ORANGE SAUCE

1½ cups (375ml, 13fl oz) orange juice

½ cup (125ml, 4fl oz) lemon juice

1 cup (220g, 8oz) caster sugar

1 tsp orange zest

2 tbsps (30ml, 1fl oz) Cointreau

Gently heat the cream and coffee for 5 minutes over a low heat. Don't overheat this mixture, it should be lukewarm to the touch.

Separate the eggs and beat the yolks with the caster sugar until they become pale. Whisk this mixture into the heated cream.

Gently stir over low heat with a spatula, stirring constantly. It will be ready once the cream coats the back of the spatula. Pour the mixture into a bowl and let cool.

Beat the egg whites with a pinch of salt until stiff peaks form. Stir them gently into the cream mixture. Refrigerate for at least 4 hours until set.

In a medium saucepan, heat orange and lemon juice and sugar over medium heat, stirring until the sugar is dissolved and the sauce thickens. The sauce should reduce by nearly half.

Let the sauce cool. Once it is cool, stir in the zest and liquor. Plate up the sauce, then the mousse and top with candied orange peel or orange slices and serve.

Apple Rose Puffs

DELICATE AND FRAGRANT, THESE DELICIOUS LITTLE PUFFS ARE MADE FOR SHARING

MAKES 6

2 tbsps lemon juice

2 red apples (try using red delicious or pink lady)

1 sheet frozen puff pastry, thawed

1 tbsp plain flour (for sprinkling over bench)

3 tbsps jam (use apricot or another 'light-flavoured' jam)

¼ tsp ground cinnamon

½ tsp icing sugar

Preheat the oven to 190°C (375°F, Gas Mark 5).

Half-fill a large microwave-proof bowl with water and the lemon juice. Cut the apples in half, remove the core and leave the peel on – this will give your puffs a lovely red trim. Slice the halves into paper-thin slices. Place each slice in the lemon water to prevent browning.

Microwave the apples in the bowl for about 3 minutes, to make them slightly softer and easy to roll. If the slices break when you bend them, then they need a little more cooking.

Place the puff pastry sheet over a clean and lightly floured bench. Using a rolling pin, gently stretch the dough into a rectangular shape of about 30 x 20cm (12 x 8in). Cut the dough in 6 strips, each about 5 x 20cm (2 x 8in).

In a small microwave-proof bowl, mix the jam with 2 tablespoons of water. Microwave for about 1 minute to make the jam easy to spread. Brush a thin layer of jam on each strip of pastry.

Drain the apple slices then arrange them lengthwise along the pastry, slightly overlapping, with the straight edge of the slices halfway down the strip.

Fold up the bottom half of the pastry strip over the apple slices. The tops of the curved edges of the slices should be sticking out above the edges of the folded pastry.

Starting from one end, gently roll the pastry, keeping the apple slices in place. Seal the edge at the end, pressing with your fingers. Place each rose puff in the depressions of a greased cupcake or muffin tray. Repeat for the other 5 roses.

Bake for about 40-45 minutes in the lower part of the oven until fully cooked. The pastry needs to be crisp all the way through.

Sprinkle with cinnamon and icing sugar.

Cocktail Party

COCKTAILS

The cocktail party comes with the expectation of a certain level of glamour: style, comfort and a chilled-out vibe are prerequisites to a successful event. While expectations can create stress, on the plus side, the lack of a seated meal helps to minimise food prep, clean up and costs.

So what do you need to do to host a successful cocktail party?

Let's start with the bar. You don't need a formal bar – a table, a kitchen bench or even a retro-style suitcase could work to present bottles. It's all about creating a look and creating space for your bottles because they are sure to get a workout on the night.

A cocktail party faux pas is to serve up your drinks in the array of misshapen and slightly damaged glasses that you have in your kitchen cupboard. Depending on the scale of the event, consider hiring glasses or perhaps purchasing plastic ones in a range of appropriate shapes and sizes.

Create an environment where people can relax, kick back and have conversations. Seating is key to this, so ensure there are plenty of places where guests can sit or lean for long periods. Lighting is important for ambience too so consider candles, lanterns and bulbs in your outdoor area. And the heart of any good party is of course music. Jazz and blues are traditional choices for a cocktail party. If music is not your thing, consider asking a friend or a professional to prepare playlists for you.

Food is important too. No need to go crazy, but remember you have a group of people in your house drinking hard liquor. Something to absorb it is definitely advisable. To keep it really simple, go with a classic combo of olives, breadsticks and dips. One step up from that, and you could add a generous cheese and meat platter. If you have the time and money to spend, then canapes are a lovely addition to a cocktail party.

Now drinks. A few tools will help make it easier: a cocktail shaker, ice cube moulds, cutting board, great knife and a juicer. You'll need plenty of ice.

It's better to have 3-4 drinks done really well than lots that aren't. Before the party, decide what drinks you are going to offer and learn how to make them. Get to know how to make the classics: a martini, a margarita, a cosmopolitan, a mohiti, manhattan and whisky sour, and choose a selection that covers off on short and long drinks and caters to the gender of your guests. You could consider a twist on a classic, perhaps a raspberry mohito or a rum manhattan. Also, have some pre-made drinks such as sangria and bottles of beer for the less cocktail-inclined. And water. Don't forget the water!

Raspberry Margarita

SERVES 6

1½ cups (185g, 6oz) fresh raspberries (frozen ones will do)

½ cup (110g, 4oz) plus 2 tsps sugar

1¼ cups (325ml, 11fl oz) water

1 cup (270ml, 9fl oz) lime juice

¾ cup (180ml, 6fl oz) orange liqueur (such as Cointreau)

¾ cup (180ml, 6fl oz) raspberry liqueur (such as Chambord)

⅓ cup (90ml, 3fl oz) tequila

Heat the raspberries, 2 teaspoons of the sugar and ¼ cup (60ml, 2fl oz) of the water over medium heat. Simmer for 15 minutes, stirring occasionally until the raspberries start to break up.

Pour the mixture into a sieve set over a bowl and push the pulp and juices through the sieve into the bowl. Place the puree in the fridge to cool.

Combine the remaining sugar and remaining water and heat in a small saucepan until the sugar is dissolved and the water is clear. Place syrup in the fridge to cool.

Mix the raspberry puree, sugar syrup, lime juice, liqueurs, and tequila in a large jug or carafe half-filled with crushed ice. Garnish the rim of your glasses with a slice of lime.

Cuba Libre

SERVES 1

2 limes

2 shots (60ml, 2fl oz) golden rum

Cola

Ice, crushed or shaved

Mint sprigs, to garnish

Squeeze the juice from 1 lime into a small bowl.

Drop half the used lime into the bowl and using a pestle press down on the skin to release some of the lime oils.

Pour the rum into a tall glass.

Slice the other lime into thin rounds and place in the glass.

Pour the lime juice over and top with shaved or crushed ice. Add cola and garnish with a sprig of mint.

GET THE LOOK

For a professional edge to your cocktails, sprinkle some salt evenly over a small plate, run a wedge of a lime around the edge of the glasses to wet the rims and place them rim-down into the salt. This will give you an edging of salt around the rim of each glass.

Campari Cocktail

SERVES 1

1 shot (30ml, 1fl oz) Campari

1 shot (30ml, 1fl oz) sweet vermouth

1 shot (30ml, 1fl oz) gin (preferably a dry or stronger style of gin)

Orange peel, to serve

Combine all of the liquid ingredients in a short glass filled with ice and stir.

To create the flamed orange peel, cut a very thin long oval slice of orange peel. Hold the short edges of the peel together with the skin facing outwards. Light a match over the top of your glass and hold the peel over it to release the oils. Don't burn or colour the peel if you can avoid it. Rub the peel gently around the rim of the glass.

After this, firmly twist the skin into a coil and drop into the drink to garnish.

Note: A plain orange peel works just as well here.

NEGRONI

The most widely accepted origin story for the Negroni comes from Florence, Italy in 1919. Count Camillo Negroni, unhappy with the strength of his regular Americano cocktail, asked the bartender to give it a kick. The worthy bartender, Fosco Scarselli, added gin instead of soda water and added an orange peel instead of lemon. And thus was the noble Negroni born.

BRUSCHETTA

Oh bruschetta, a simple little dish so misunderstood and so riddled with potential pitfalls.

First among them is pronunciation. It's Italian, not German, so it's pronounced broo-SKEH-tah, not broo-SHEH-tah. Glad we got that cleared up.

Next is the bigger question of what exactly it is, how it should be made, and what is permissible to put on it.

Bruschetta is a form of antipasto from Italy that consists of bread rubbed with garlic and olive oil. That's easy.

How should it be made and what is permissible to put on it are two parts of the same dilemma. It seems that some of us can't cope with the simplicity of bruschetta and insist on topping it with everything from mushrooms to pesto to ricotta to honey, much to the outrage of the traditionalists.

Traditionalists have a point though, because it's thought that bruschetta has a pretty long tradition. It goes way, way back to the Etruscan age when farmers, while occupying the land between Rome and Tuscany, began brushing slices of the local, salt-less bread (best when it's a day old and a little bit stale) with a clove of garlic and a drizzle of olive oil and baking them in ovens. Farmers believed the oil should be quite young for the best flavour. They also believed it should be consumed with a good glass of wine, hence the Italian rule 'Day-old bread, month-old oil and year-old wine'. This combination of slightly stale bread and young olive oil is at the heart of bruschetta and for many people it's enough. But, to be fair, this basic recipe has evolved over centuries with regional variations in Italy that form the basis of today's popular versions.

In Naples, bruschetta is served with tomatoes. Good tomatoes. Chopped into small pieces and sprinkled with salt and herbs perhaps. In Rome, they like anchovies and mozzarella. In Calabria, pepper and oregano is added. In many parts of Tuscany, bruschetta, also known there as *fettunta* ('greased slice') is served with meats such as sausage, parma ham or even chicken livers.

So when you think about it, modern-day fancy variations are just another evolution and not such a violation after all.

Even though tomato is not always served on bruschetta, when it is, most people would agree that the type of tomato is essential to the dish. Choose the reddest, freshest, juiciest beefsteak or roma tomatoes you can find, and you can't go too far wrong.

Bruschetta is great on the barbecue as the slightly charred or smoky taste complements the simplicity of the dish.

Lemon Bruschetta

SERVES 4

1 French bread stick

¼ cup (50ml, 2fl oz) extra virgin olive oil

1 garlic clove, minced

½ tbsp lemon juice

½ tsp lemon zest

150g (5oz) mixed salad greens, finely chopped

250g (9oz) soft feta or cream cheese

Slice the bread stick diagonally into 1cm (½ in) thick rounds.

In a small bowl, mix together the olive oil, minced garlic, lemon juice and zest.

Brush both sides of each bread slice generously with the oil mix.

Place under a hot grill, on a grill pan, or in a frying pan and lightly toast until golden brown on each side.

Spread the feta or cream cheese generously onto each slice and top with the chopped salad greens.

Green Olive Tapenade

SERVES 4

2 garlic cloves, minced

Juice and grated zest of ½ lemon

1 tbsp salted capers, soaked in water for 10 minutes, drained and rinsed

8 white anchovy fillets in oil, drained

2 tsps fresh thyme leaves, chopped

350g (14oz) pitted green olives

¼ cup (60g, 2oz) Greek yoghurt

¼ cup (60ml, 2 fl oz) extra virgin olive oil

Freshly ground black pepper

Blend the garlic, lemon juice and zest, capers, anchovies, and thyme in a food processor or with a blender stick until well mixed. Add the olives and yoghurt and pulse to a coarse paste. Slowly pour in the oil, blending as you go, until it's the texture you like – you may not need all the oil.

Taste and add black pepper if necessary.

Red Onion Jam

SWEET, GOOEY AND COMFORTING, THIS JAM IS THE
PERFECT ACCOMPANIMENT FOR MEATS, CHEESE AND FRUIT

SERVES 6

2 tbsps olive oil

4 large red onions, finely sliced

1 garlic clove, minced

⅔ cup (100g, 3oz) brown sugar, firmly packed

½ tbsp Dijon mustard

1 tsp salt

¼ tsp black pepper

¼ tsp dried thyme

¼ cup (60ml, 2fl oz) red wine vinegar

¼ cup (60ml, 2fl oz) balsamic vinegar

Heat the olive oil in a medium frying pan. Add the onions and garlic and saute over a low heat for about 25 minutes until softened.

Stir in the brown sugar, mustard, salt, pepper and thyme and cook uncovered over low heat, stirring occasionally, for about 15 minutes, ensuring all the sugar is dissolved.

Add the vinegars and simmer for a further 20 minutes or so, stirring occasionally until the mixture is thickened to a jam-like consistency. (It will thicken further once cooled.)

Bottle into a sterilised jar and seal while hot.

Store in the fridge after opening. The jam should be good for up to 3 weeks.

Prawn Toast with Lemon-Thyme Sauce

LIGHT, COLOURFUL AND FRESH, THIS IS A GREAT CHOICE OF CANAPE FOR YOUR SUMMER COCKTAIL PARTY

MAKES 12

SAUCE

1 cup (250g, 8oz) Greek yoghurt

½ cup (125ml, 4fl oz) whole-egg mayonnaise

Finely grated zest and juice of 1 lemon (about 1 tsp zest and 2 to 3 tbsps juice)

½ tbsp fresh dill leaves, chopped

½ tbsp fresh thyme leaves, chopped

Coarse salt and ground pepper

TOASTS

3 large slices wholemeal bread, crusts removed

¼ cup (60ml, 2fl oz) olive oil

12 raw prawn tails

Salt and pepper

Olives, to garnish

Thyme, to garnish

In a small bowl, combine yoghurt, mayonnaise, lemon zest and juice, dill and thyme; season with salt and pepper.

Lightly brush each side of the bread with 1 tablespoon of the olive oil. Place slices under a hot grill, on a grill pan, or in a frying pan and lightly toast until golden brown on each side. Cut each slice into quarter squares.

In a small bowl, drizzle the remaining olive oil over the prawn tails and season liberally with salt and pepper and toss to coat the prawns.

Heat a frying pan on medium-high heat. Fry the prawns for 5 minutes each, turning once halfway.

Place a dollop of the sauce in the centre of each toast square and place a cooked prawn on top.

Garnish with the fresh thyme and olives.

Herring with Slaw on Rye Toasts

SO PRETTY — PLUS THIS SCANDINAVIAN-STYLE PICKLED HERRING CAN BE MADE NOW AND IT WILL KEEP FOR WEEKS

SERVES 4

PICKLED HERRING

8 salted herring fillets

2 cups (500ml, 1pt) white vinegar

¾ cup (165g, 6oz) sugar

2 bay leaves

1 carrot, roughly chopped

1 onion, sliced

2 tsps whole black peppercorns

1 tsp yellow mustard seeds

Salt and ground pepper, to taste

SLAW

¼ head red cabbage, shredded

3 medium beetroots, grated

2 medium carrots, grated

1 bulb fennel, finely sliced

2 tbsps fresh parsley leaves, chopped

Juice of ½ to 1 lemon, to taste

2 tbsps maple syrup

Salt and pepper

4 slices of rye bread

¼ cup (60ml, 2fl oz) olive oil

To make the pickled herring, rinse the herring fillets and place in a bowl. Cover with water and transfer to the fridge to soak overnight.

Combine all the ingredients for the pickling liquid in a medium saucepan and bring to a boil over medium-high heat. Reduce heat and simmer for 5 minutes, or until the sugar has dissolved. Remove from heat and set aside to cool to room temperature.

Drain the herring fillets and place in a stainless steel, ceramic or glass bowl. Pour in the cooled pickling liquid and stir to combine. Cover and set aside in a cool place to marinate for 2 days.

Next make the slaw. Combine the vegetables and parsley in a large bowl and drizzle over the lemon juice and maple syrup. Toss to mix thoroughly, adding salt and pepper as needed.

Allow your slaw to stand for around 20 minutes before serving, tossing regularly.

Lightly brush each side of the bread slices with olive oil.

Place slices under a hot grill, on a grill pan, or in a frying pan and lightly toast until golden brown on each side. Cut each slice into half.

Place a dessertspoon of the slaw on each piece of rye toast and flatten slightly. Place a small piece of the pickled herring on top and serve.

Greek-Style Mini Lamb Sliders

THESE FRESH AND TASTY SLIDERS ARE THE PERFECT PARTY SNACK

SERVES 15

TZATZIKI SAUCE

1 cucumber, peeled and seeded

2 garlic cloves, minced

1 tsp lemon zest

¼ cup (10g, ¼ oz) fresh dill, finely chopped

1¼ cups (310g, 10oz) Greek yoghurt

1 tbsp white wine vinegar

2 tbsps extra virgin olive oil

1½ tsps salt

⅛ tsp black pepper

1¼ cup (210g, 8oz) green peas (fresh or frozen)

700g, (1½ lb) leg of lamb, boneless, trimmed

¼ cup (60ml, 2fl oz) olive oil

1 tbsp salt

¼ tsp ground pepper

15 mini pitas

Preheat oven to 150°C (300°F, Gas Mark 2).

Grate the cucumber then place into a colander with a pinch of salt. Let sit for 15 minutes then squeeze out the excess liquid.

Place grated cucumber, garlic, lemon zest and dill in a medium-sized bowl. Add the yoghurt, vinegar, olive oil, salt and pepper and mix well. Set aside.

Cook the peas in a saucepan of boiling water. Drain and set aside to cool slightly, then mash gently with the back of a spoon.

Slice lamb into thick slices. Transfer to a bowl and add the olive oil, salt and pepper. Toss to coat.

Heat a grill pan over medium heat, then brush with oil. Grill lamb for 3 minutes on either side. Set aside to rest. When rested, slice into thinner strips.

Meanwhile, prepare the pitas. Cut in half and wrap in foil then transfer to the oven for 10 minutes to warm through.

To prepare, fill the pitas with tzatziki, smashed peas and lamb.

Gourmet Cheese Balls

THESE SOFT, CRUNCHY, CHEWY BALLS MAKE A DELICIOUS DAIRY-FREE ALTERNATIVE TO AFTER DINNER CHEESE AND CRACKERS

SERVES 12

1½ cups (185g, 6oz) raw cashews, soaked for 4hrs, drained and rinsed

3 tbsps coconut oil

1 tbsp white wine

½ lemon, juiced

¼ tsp sea salt

Warm water, as needed

3 tbsps dried cranberries, chopped

¼ cup (30g, 1oz) walnuts, chopped

TOPPINGS

½ cup (60g, 2oz) walnuts, roughly chopped

½ cup (50g, 2oz) dried cranberries, roughly chopped

1 cup (45g, 1½ oz) flat-leaf parsley, roughly chopped

Place the cashews, coconut oil, wine, lemon juice and salt into a high-speed blender and process until smooth. If the mixture is too thick to blend, gradually add warm water a teaspoon at a time.

Add the cranberries and the walnuts and pulse for 5-10 seconds until just combined. Scrape into a large bowl, cover, and transfer to the freezer to chill for 15 minutes to firm up slightly.

Line a baking tray or plate with baking paper. Set aside.

Prepare a clean and dry chopping board or work surface and sprinkle with the toppings.

Remove cheese from the freezer and, using damp hands, roll into balls of equal size.

Roll each ball through the toppings until completely covered.

Place balls on the prepared tray and transfer to the freezer to chill for 1 hour before serving.

WHAT IS THIS SOFT CHEESE ANYWAY?

Perhaps you've had a moment at a party or friend's place for dinner, when you popped a morsel in your mouth featuring a soft white cheese and you thought to yourself 'What exactly was that?' There are many possibilities, from the humble cream cheese to the popular ricotta to the less well-known but increasingly popular labna, curd (cow's or goat's) or quark.

CREAM CHEESE

Cream cheese is so common that you probably never stopped to think what's actually in it. The clue is in the name perhaps. Yes, cream cheese is a combination of cream and cheese, but it probably also has some stabilisers added, such as carob gum, in industrial production. Cream cheese is a party favourite going way back. It's a core component of many dips and spreads and it provides the basis for delicious cream-cheese frosting common on carrot cake and, of course, is central to any good cheesecake.

LABNA

Labna is a staple of Middle Eastern cuisine. It might sound unusual if you are not used to it, but its just salted yoghurt that has had the whey (liquid part) extracted. The resultant 'cheese' is thick, creamy, salty and delicious. It's actually really easy to make at home if you fancy giving it a try, and it's also one of the more healthy of these cheeses as it's packed full of probiotics or 'good bacteria'.

CURD

Curd seems to have come from nowhere replacing yoghurt on menus at trendy cafes, although it's definitely nothing new in India where it's been at the heart of many dishes for centuries. But what exactly is the difference between yoghurt and curd? It comes down to the technique of production and without getting too technical about it, curd contains only lactic acid bacteria – it is made by adding lactic acid or lemon juice to boiling milk – whereas yoghurt contains multiple types of bacteria which are generally added to the milk during production. Both can be sweetened or unsweetened before fermentation.

QUARK

Quark is yet another dairy product with similarities to all of the above. Quark is the German name for this soft, curd cheese. Quark is made by warming soured milk (traditionally the milk was allowed to sour naturally and this is one difference between it and curd) and then straining it. It has a little more liquid whey present than the others.

All clear now?

Salmon Canapes

MAKES 12

170g (6oz) cream cheese, room temperature

2 tbsps plain Greek yoghurt

170g (6oz) smoked salmon

12 mini crackers

4 tbsps dill, finely chopped

Salt and fresh ground pepper

In a medium bowl, beat the cream cheese and yoghurt until light and fluffy.

Cut the salmon into 12 squares large enough to wrap over the filling.

Cover each cracker with a generous sprinkle of dill leaving plenty at the edges of the cracker.

Spoon a ball of cream cheese mixture (you can use a melon baller for this if you have one) on top of the herbs. Make sure it is nice and plump to give height to the canape.

Next fold the salmon squares over the top of each cracker and tuck in gently at the base.

Salmon Wraps

MAKES 12

12 slices smoked salmon, 8 x 6cm (3 x 2½in)

¾ cup (90g, 3oz) goat's cheese

1 cup (30g, 1oz) rocket leaves

1 lemon, cut into wedges, to garnish

Place 1 slice of salmon on your work surface.

Spread about 2 teaspoons of the goat's cheese along one edge of the slice. Make sure you've got it right to the edge of the salmon.

Place 2 or 3 leaves of rocket over the cheese, so that a small part of the leaves are overhanging each end of the salmon.

Starting with the end that has the cheese along it, carefully roll up the slice. Place on your serving dish so that the overlapping end of the roll is on the bottom.

Repeat with the other slices of salmon.

Squeeze some lemon over for garnish.

DILL

Dill is a flavour-packed herb that is commonly used in Eastern European dishes. Dill is used with soups, eggs, cucumbers, potatoes, fish and, of course, pickles. Fresh dill is also great in garden salads –either chopped and mixed through or added to the salad dressing. Dill comes from the carrot family and has the same light, wispy appearance as carrot leaves. It is best used fresh as it loses it flavour and aroma once dried. The dill seeds can also be used in cooking as a spice, and taste similar to caraway seeds.

Chicken and Cream Cheese Sushi Rolls

THESE CREAMY GREEN SUSHI ROLLS ARE A REAL WINNER WITH KIDS AS WELL AS ADULTS

SERVES 6 (MAKES APPROX 15 SUSHI ROLLS)

SUSHI RICE

5 tbsps rice wine vinegar

1½ tsps fine sea salt

2 tbsps sugar

3 cups (465g, 12oz) sushi rice

3½ cups (875ml, 30fl oz) cold water

SUSHI ROLLS

5 sheets of nori

150g (5oz) cream cheese

3-4 leaves butter lettuce

1 cucumber, julienned

1 chicken breast, poached and sliced

¾ cup (25g, 1oz) finely chopped coriander and dill, for rolling

To make the sushi rice, gently warm the rice wine vinegar in a small saucepan over a low heat. Add salt and sugar and whisk until fully dissolved. Set aside.

Place the rice in a large colander and rinse under a cold tap 8-10 times as required until the water runs completely clear. Transfer the rice to a large bowl and cover with water. Set aside to soak for 30 minutes. Rinse and drain.

Place rice and cold water in a large covered saucepan over a medium-high heat. Use a heavy lid or weigh down the lid with a heatproof object. When rice boils immediately reduce the heat to low and allow to simmer for precisely 20 minutes – use a kitchen timer as cooking time is important. Remove the lid and remove the pan from the heat.

Transfer the rice to a large, wide mixing bowl. Use a spoon to gently spread and separate the grains, enabling it to cool slightly.

Drizzle the rice seasoning over the warm rice while gently turning the grains over and over. Try not to stir the rice or squash it. Set aside to cool slightly – sushi rice should be at room temperature when rolled. Do not refrigerate.

Set your sushi mat on a clean work surface with the slats running horizontally top and bottom. Place a nori sheet on top, shiny-side down, leaving a gap at the edge closest to you. Dampen your hands in warm water and then spread a thin layer of rice evenly over the nori sheet using your hands, leaving a space about the width of two fingers along the edge furthest from you.

Spread cream cheese in a horizontal line along the centre of the sushi roll, then add the butter lettuce, cucumber and chicken pieces.

Use your thumbs and forefingers to hold the edge of the mat and your other fingers to keep the filling in place while rolling the mat over. Gently pull the mat as you go to create a firm roll. Continue rolling evenly until all the rice is covered with the nori. Moisten the edge of the nori with water and gently squeeze shut. Using a very sharp knife moistened with water, slice the sushi roll into even pieces.

Sprinkle the chopped herbs onto a work surface. Gently roll each piece of sushi in the herbs to ensure an even covering.

Turkey Meatballs with Ginger Sauce

PERFECT PARTY FOOD THAT IS SIMPLE AND QUICK TO MAKE,
FUSS-FREE TO EAT, AND GREAT FOR SHARING

MAKES 24

MEATBALLS

¼ cup (30g, 1oz) breadcrumbs

¼ cup (60ml, 2fl oz) milk

1.5 kg (3lb 5oz) turkey mince

1 tbsp garlic, minced

2 tsp fresh ginger, minced

2 tbsps spring onion, minced

2 tbsps soy sauce

¼ cup (40g, 1½ oz) canned pineapple, drained

¼ tsp pepper

SAUCE

½ cup (125ml, 4fl oz) soy sauce

¼ cup (60ml, 2fl oz) water

¼ cup (60ml, 2fl oz) pineapple juice

¼ cup (40g, 1½ oz) brown sugar

2 tsps garlic, minced

1 tsp fresh ginger, minced

2 tsps cornflour

Sesame seeds

Preheat oven to 245°C (475°F, Gas Mark 9) and spray a baking tray with cooking spray.

Mix the breadcrumbs in the milk and allow to soak for 5 minutes.

In a large bowl, combine turkey, garlic, ginger, spring onions, soy sauce, pineapple and pepper, then add the soaked breadcrumbs.

Using your hands, combine the mixture and shape into small balls using around 3 tablespoons of mixture for each ball. Place meatballs on the tray and bake for 14 minutes until fully cooked.

Meanwhile, prepare the sauce by whisking together the soy sauce, water, pineapple juice, brown sugar, garlic and ginger in a medium saucepan over medium heat. Whisk constantly until the sugar has dissolved.

In a new bowl, whisk cornflour with a tablespoon of water. Stir this cornflour slurry into the sauce and simmer for 5 minutes, until it has a thick syrup consistency.

Remove meatballs from oven. Place in a large serving bowl and serve with sauce poured over top and sprinkled with sesame seeds, or on a platter with sauce for dipping on the side.

Mini Pizzas

PARTY FOOD DOESN'T COME MUCH BETTER THAN THIS. CRUNCHY, GOOEY MINI PIZZAS THAT ALL YOUR GUESTS WILL LOVE

SERVES 6

PIZZA BASES

2 cups (250g, 8oz) baker's (or plain) flour

7g (¼ oz) sachet dry active yeast

1 tsp caster sugar

1 tsp salt

¾ cup (200ml, 7fl oz) warm water

1 tbsp olive oil, plus extra to grease

TOPPING

⅔ cup (160ml, 5fl oz) passata

¼ zucchini, finely diced

1 tbsp fresh (or dried) oregano, finely chopped

1 cup (125g, 4oz) mozzarella cheese, grated

Sift flour into a large mixing bowl. Stir in yeast, sugar and salt. Make a well in the centre and pour in water and oil. Bring the dough together with your hands. Turn out onto a lightly floured surface and knead for 5 minutes by hand (or use an electric mixer with a dough hook) until the dough is smooth. Separate the dough into 6 pieces and roll into small dough balls.

Clean the bowl for reuse. Lightly grease the cleaned bowl with a little oil, then add dough balls and cover with a tea towel or plastic wrap. Set aside in a warm place to prove for 1 hour, until doubled in size.

Preheat oven to 240°C (465°F, Gas Mark 9). Lightly flour a large baking tray.

Knock back the dough by punching it to remove air and divide into 2 balls. Roll dough out on a lightly floured surface to create a thin base. Transfer to prepared baking tray.

Cover bases with passata, zucchini and oregano, then sprinkle cheese generously over the top.

Transfer to the oven and and bake for 10 minutes until cheese has melted and the pizza bases are crisp and golden around the edges.

Creamy Potato Croquettes

CRUNCHY ON THE OUTSIDE, CREAMY ON THE INSIDE, THIS FINGER FOOD IS A GREAT WAY TO KICK OFF YOUR PARTY

SERVES 6

4 medium potatoes, peeled

110g (4oz) butter

1 cup (125g, 4oz) plain flour

2 cups (500ml, 1pt) milk, at room temperature

2 cups (475ml, 1pt) cream, at room temperature

60g (2oz) butter, cut into cubes

1 egg, slightly beaten, in a shallow bowl

¼ cup (30g, 1oz) breadcrumbs, in a shallow bowl

¼ cup (60ml, 2fl oz) olive oil

Chop the potatoes into even-sized pieces so they cook at the same rate.

Place potatoes in a large saucepan and cover with cold, salted water. Bring to a boil over a high heat. Reduce heat slightly and cook for 10 minutes or until a knife easily pierces through the potato. Strain and return potatoes to the pan, mash them and cover with a lid to keep warm.

Next make the bechamel sauce. First melt the butter in a medium saucepan over a medium heat, then slowly add the flour stirring continuously. Cook the flour for 5 minutes until a smooth golden paste forms. Begin to slowly add the milk and cream, alternating between each addition. Stir constantly to ensure no lumps form. It can take around 20 minutes of stirring and cooking to create a nice, smooth bechamel.

At this stage, add the warm mashed potatoes to the pan and begin to blend using an immersion blender. Gradually add the cubes of butter until fully incorporated.

Transfer the mixture to the fridge and allow to cool completely. You can make this mixture in the morning, and allow several hours for cooling if you like.

About 90 minutes before cooking, remove the mixture from the fridge and form into rolls using your hands. Dip the croquettes in beaten egg and roll in breadcrumbs. Return to the fridge for an hour before cooking.

When ready to cook, remove the croquettes from the fridge. Heat the oil in a large frying pan over a high heat and fry the croquettes until crispy and golden.

Allow to drain on paper towels before serving garnished with fresh herbs.

ROSE WATER

Roses are commonly harvested for their oil, which is an expensive and desirable perfume, while rose water is usually the byproduct of making the oil. A beautiful byproduct it is though, and one that has a solid and growing market among home cooks and restaurateurs.

You can make it yourself, although you'll need a lot of time and roses (about 1kg to make 1L of rose water!). The variety of rose water that you buy at the supermarket will likely have been flavoured with rose oil or essence, but that's just fine too.

COOKING WITH ROSE WATER

Rose water is a staple and somewhat evocative ingredient in Middle Eastern cuisine. Pair it with pistachio nuts for an authentic Arabian vibe. It used to be much more commonplace in European cuisine too, until the advent of vanilla, which stole the show somewhat. It's making a resurgence though and it's easy to see why. It's such a beautiful ingredient that adds a perfectly soft floral note to any dish. It feels fresh and sophisticated and guests will appreciate its delicacy and flavour.

Commonly rose water is used to flavour cakes or biscuits such as shortbread or the madaleines featured on the next page of this book. It goes very nicely with creamy ingredients, so think panacotta, cheesecake, ice cream or rice pudding. It's less common in savoury dishes but tagines and rice pilaf provide opportunities to use rose water as part of your main meal.

ACCESSORISING WITH ROSE WATER

As well as an ingredient, you could think of rose water as a way to accessorise your food. Put some rose water into a spray bottle and spritz over a glass of prosecco or a bowl of fresh strawberries, for example.

You can also use rose water as a last-minute flavouring, to refresh or add an extra dimension to a plain ingredient. It's lovely used to flavour cream, yoghurt or honey – just add a few drops before serving. Or how about adding rose water to your salad dressing? It goes beautifully with a carroty or nutty salad.

You could consider taking inspiration from rose water by using roses to present your food. They make beautiful decorations and a neat way to present them is frozen in ice cubes, as in the photograph opposite. As the ice melts, little rose petals will float in your diners' drinks – so pretty.

Rose Water Madeleines

SOFT, DELICATE, FLOWER-FILLED BISCUITS, BEAUTIFULLY
PRESENTED AND PERFECT FOR A GIRLS' NIGHT

MAKES 24

2 eggs

½ cup (110g, 4oz) sugar

1 tsp vanilla extract

2 tsps rose water

1 cup (125g, 4oz) plain flour

¼ tsp salt

¼ tsp baking powder

125g (4oz) butter, melted

GLAZE

1 cup (160g, 5oz) icing sugar

1 tsp butter, melted

2 tbsps lemon juice

Rose petals, chopped, to serve (optional)

Preheat the oven to 180°C (350°F, Gas Mark 4) and lightly grease two 12-hole madeleine pans.

Using an electric mixer on a high speed, cream eggs and sugar for 3-4 minutes until light and fluffy.

Add vanilla, rose water, flour, salt and baking powder. Reduce mixer speed to low and slowly pour in the melted butter. Mix until well incorporated but not over-worked.

Divide batter evenly in the pans then transfer to the oven to bake for about 10 minutes or until golden and darkening around the edges.

Remove from the oven and cool for 5 minutes, then invert onto a wire rack to cool completely.

While the madeleines are cooking, make the glaze. Sift icing sugar into a small heatproof bowl. Stir in the butter and just enough lemon juice to make a thick paste. Place the bowl over a small saucepan of simmering water and cook, stirring constantly, until icing is of a pouring consistency. Pour icing into a piping bag (or use a ziplock bag). Release the nozzle from the piping bag or cut a small nick in the corner of the ziplock bag, and ice the madeleines by quickly moving the piping bag over the top in a zig-zag pattern.

Scatter with rose petals for a pretty finish.

Mint Chocolate Truffles

THESE RICH AND SUMPTUOUS TRUFFLES ARE THE IDEAL AFTER DINNER MINT. SIT BACK, RELAX AND REWARD YOURSELF FOR A JOB WELL DONE

MAKES 8

350g (12oz) dark chocolate (minimum 60% cacao content), finely chopped

1¼ cups (310ml, 10fl oz) heavy whipping cream

2 cups (90g, 3oz) firmly packed fresh mint leaves, rinsed and patted dry

⅓ cup (35g, 1oz) unsweetened cocoa powder

Line a square or rectangular baking tray with aluminum foil leaving a slight overhang.

Place the chocolate in a medium-sized bowl.

Place the cream in a small saucepan and bring to the boil over a medium-high heat. Add the mint leaves and stir. Cover the saucepan with a lid and remove from the heat. Set aside to steep for 20 minutes and then remove the mint leaves using a slotted spoon.

Return the cream to the heat and again bring to a gentle boil. Pour the cream over the chocolate, and allow to stand for 30 seconds before stirring together until completely combined and very smooth.

Pour the mixture into the baking tray, making sure the mixture reaches in the corners. Cover the tray tightly with plastic wrap and transfer to the fridge to cool for about 1 hour until the mixture is firm but not very hard.

Lift the mixture from the pan using the overhanging edges of foil. Carefully cut the truffle mixture (using a ruler if you want precise and equal squares) into small blocks of the desired size. If the truffles have become soft from being out of the fridge, cover and return to the fridge.

Line an airtight container with baking paper.

Sift the cocoa powder into a medium-sized bowl. Remove the truffles from the fridge and quickly roll them in the cocoa being careful not to nudge the edges or otherwise damage the square shape. Shake off excess cocoa powder and place the squares into the container. Secure the lid and return to the fridge until ready to eat.

Serve the truffle squares at room temperature.

Clementine Macarons with White Chocolate Ganache

MASTER THESE DELECTIBLE CITRUS MACARONS AND YOU'LL BE THE BELLE OF THE BALL!

MAKES 30

SHELLS

1¾ cups (210g, 8oz) almond meal

1½ cups (210g, 8oz) icing sugar

3 clementines (or oranges), finely zested

3 egg whites

2 drops orange food colouring

1½ cups (235g, 8oz) sugar

⅔ cup (160ml, 5fl oz) water

GANACHE

300g (10oz) white chocolate, finely chopped

¾ cup (185ml, 6fl oz) heavy cream

1 tsp vanilla extract

Preheat the oven to 180°C (350°F, Gas Mark 4) and line three baking trays with greaseproof paper.

In a medium bowl, blend together the almond meal, icing sugar, clementine zest and 2 tablespoons of egg white and blend to form a paste.

In an electric mixer, whisk the egg white and food colouring until foamy. Keep the machine running on a very low speed for the next step.

In a saucepan over a medium-high heat, stir together sugar and water. Using a thermometer heat the mixture to 120°C (250°F) and then immediately remove from the heat and pour down the side of the mixing bowl into the beaten egg whites. Increase the speed to high and beat until a thick meringue has formed.

Gently fold meringue into the almond meal mixture in three batches. Transfer to a piping bag and pipe rounds onto a baking tray about 5cm (2in) apart. Repeat until batter has all been used.

Place in the oven and bake for 10 minutes until tops have hardened. Allow to cool for 5 minutes before transferring to a wire rack.

Put the chopped white chocolate in a medium heatproof mixing bowl and set aside. Place the cream and vanilla extract in a small saucepan over a low heat until it begins to simmer. Immediately pour the cream over the chocolate and let it sit for 2-3 minutes. Stir to combine.

To assemble, match the shells together in pairs. Pipe a small round of ganache on the flat side of one macaron shell. Top with the other matching macaron shell.

Espresso Cocktail

THIS FLAVOUR-PACKED DRINK COMBINES TWO OF LIFE'S
ESSENTIALS: COFFEE AND ALCOHOL

SERVES 1

2 shots (60ml, 2fl oz)
vodka

1 shot (30ml, 1fl oz)
coffee liqueur (like
Kahlua or Baileys)

1 shot (30ml, 1fl oz)
espresso

Coffee beans, for
garnish

Chill a martini glass (leave in the fridge or fill it with ice).

Pour the vodka, liqueur and espresso into a cocktail shaker with
fresh ice, and shake well (if you can, shake vigorously enough so
that you get a bit of foam). Strain your cocktail into the chilled
glass.

Top with a few coffee beans and serve.

Winter Warmers

MAKING A MEAL OF SALADS

Salads have undergone a facelift in recent years. Long gone is the notion of a salad as a bit of limp lettuce and tomato on the side, or a dutiful munch through too-much-green-stuff. In fact, salads have strayed so far from our original notion of salad that it may make the philosophically minded wonder what makes a salad a salad!

One enduring definition of salad is that it needs to be 'cold' or raw, so we are pushing the definition even by speaking about warm salads. But, never mind, warm salads are a thing, they are here, and they are a great option to pair with dinner on a winter night, or even to make into dinner itself – they can certainly be substantial enough for that.

Warm salads are as diverse and varied as any main meal, but there are a few common factors that seem to shift a salad from an 'on the side' position on the table to a main element.

MEAT AND FISH

One factor is the addition of meat. Add a nicely grilled steak or piece of tender pink lamb to your salad ingredients and it instantly feels like a meal. A chargrilled piece of steak pairs nicely with both Italian and Asian flavourings, then all you need to do is add some greens and a suitable dressing. Don't forget about seafood as a salad option.

Prawns, crab and calamari all make a great base for a dinner salad.

ROASTING

Another factor is roasting. As soon as you pile a heap of veggies together into a roasting tin with olive oil and seasonings, you are transforming them from something on the side to a substantial meal. Scatter with feta cheese or blue cheese, and you have a bit of protein to add to your supper too.

PULSES AND CARBOHYDRATES

The other element that bulks up a salad, taking it to the next level, is the inclusion of some form of pulse or carbohydrate. Pasta salad is an old fave, but also think Asian noodle salad – full of great flavours and textures – or a salad that uses warm pearl barley, buckwheat or quinoa as a base.

There's a great Italian salad called panzanella that combines crunchy fried bread with mozzarella and tomatoes for a satisfying salad that works for main or entree. Lentils are another handy base to have for a salad – they are great paired with Indian spices, as well as nuts and cheese.

These ingredients provide texture, taste and substance to any salad, catapulting it from support act to the lead role in your dinner menu.

Warm Caprese Salad with Home-Made Pesto

TRANSFORM THIS CLASSIC ITALIAN SALAD FOR A WINTER'S NIGHT — A GREAT ACCOMPANIMENT TO PASTA

SERVES 4

PESTO

1 cup (30g, 1oz) basil leaves (retain a few leaves to garnish)

¼ cup (30g, 1oz) pine nuts, toasted

¼ cup (60ml, 2fl oz) olive oil

1 garlic clove, crushed

½ tsp salt

¼ tsp pepper

¼ cup (30g, 1oz) Parmesan, grated

SALAD

20 mini vine-ripened tomatoes (still on the vine)

Olive oil

½ tsp sea salt

200g (7oz) burrata (if you can get it) or regular fresh mozzarella or buffalo mozzarella, sliced

First make the pesto. Place the basil, pine nuts, olive oil, garlic, salt and pepper into a food processor and pulse until smooth. Add the Parmesan and pulse until a thicker consistency is reached. Cover and place in the fridge until ready.

Next, slow roast the tomatoes. Preheat the oven to 180°C (350°F, Gas Mark 4). Place the tomatoes, still on the vine, into a baking dish and drizzle with olive oil. Sprinkle over the sea salt. Transfer to the oven to roast for 25 minutes or until tomatoes are shrunken and soft, but not brown.

To serve, place the cheese on the plate, topped with a generous spoonful of pesto and finished with the vine tomatoes and some fresh basil, to garnish.

Wild Winter Salad

A DELICIOUS, NUTRITIOUS SALAD THAT'S GOT TEXTURE AND
TASTE TO SURPRISE AND DELIGHT YOUR GUESTS

SERVES 4

3¼ cups (810ml, 26fl oz) salted water or vegetable stock

1 cup (155g, 4oz) long grain brown rice

½ cup (80g, 3oz) wild rice

1kg (2lb) butternut pumpkin, peeled and cut into chunks

½ tsp salt

½ tsp pepper

1 tbsp olive oil

1 tbsp butter

400g (14oz) flat mushrooms, quartered

¾ cup (75g, 3oz) pecans

1 tbsp maple syrup

½ tsp sea salt

½ cup (20g, ¾ oz) parsley, chopped

Preheat the oven to 200°C (400°F, Gas Mark 6).

Place the water or stock in a medium saucepan and bring to the boil. Add the brown rice and wild rice, cover and simmer for 50 minutes. Remove from heat, and set aside for 10 minutes before fluffing with a fork.

Spread the pumpkin out on a baking tray lined with baking paper and sprinkle with salt, pepper and olive oil. Transfer to the oven to roast for 35 minutes until tender.

Meanwhile, line a separate baking tray with baking paper. Toss the pecans in maple syrup and sea salt, then roast for 12 minutes or until golden. Cool completely on tray.

Heat the butter in a frying pan and add mushrooms. Cook, stirring occasionally, for 4 minutes or until mushrooms are tender.

Place cooked rice, pumpkin, mushrooms and pecans in a bowl and gently mix to combine. Turn onto plates and scatter with chopped parsley to serve.

Spicy Pepitas

SERVES 6 (YIELD 2 CUPS)

1¾ cups (215g, 7oz) pepitas

6 garlic cloves, minced

1 tsp chilli powder

1 tsp cayenne pepper

½ tsp salt

4 tsps sugar

1 lime, juiced

Dry fry the pepitas in a large frying pan over a medium-high heat until they begin to pop.

Add the garlic and continue to stir until garlic and seeds are browned but not burned. Remove from the heat and then stir in chilli powder, cayenne pepper and salt. Stir for 10-20 seconds until well coated.

Transfer to a large mixing bowl and add the sugar. Stir to combine. Add the lime juice and again stir to coat the pepitas thoroughly.

Spread mixture onto a baking tray and set aside until dry. It's ideal to leave the seeds to crisp up overnight, but for a minimum of 5 hours will be enough. Stir every 30 minutes for the first 3 hours. When dry, store in airtight container until ready to serve.

Honeyed Nuts & Pumpkin

SERVES 2

120g (4oz) butter

¼ cup (60ml, 2fl oz) maple syrup

1 tsp cumin

½ cup (60g, 2oz) walnuts and blanched almonds

Sea salt and cracked pepper

1kg (2lb) pumpkin, cut into cubes

Preheat the oven to 200°C (400°F, Gas Mark 6).

Melt the butter in a medium saucepan over a medium-high heat. Add the maple syrup, cumin, nuts, salt and pepper and stir to combine.

Line a roasting tray with baking paper and add the pumpkin.

Pour the maple syrup mixture over the pumpkin and toss or turn to ensure evenly coated.

Place in the oven to roast for 30 minutes or until pumpkin is very tender and sauce has caramelised.

SUNFLOWER SEEDS

Sunflower seeds come from the beautiful bright yellow sunflower, and are not only a great source of nutrition but also delicious on their own or as a meal topping. These versatile seeds can be toasted and seasoned with savoury flavours to add to salads, or used raw in breads, smoothies, eggs and pestos. They add a delicious nutty taste to every dish and are high in nutritional value. Sunflower seeds are packed full of vitamins and minerals, including Vitamin E, magnesium and folate, plus they are low in carbohydrates so you don't have to worry about your waistline!

TIP: Keep your sunflower seeds in an airtight container in the fridge to keep them fresh longer.

Cauliflower Steaks

SCOTCH FILLET FOR THE VEGETARIANS, THESE MEATY, TASTY CAULIFLOWER STEAKS ARE PLEASINGLY SUBSTANTIAL

SERVES 4

SALSA VERDE

1 cup (30g, 1oz) parsley leaves

½ cup (20g, ¾ oz) coriander leaves

½ cup (20g, ¾ oz) mint leaves

½ cup (20g, ¾ oz) spring onion, roughly chopped

1 garlic clove, peeled and crushed

1 lemon, juiced

⅓ cup (80ml, 3fl oz) olive oil

CAULIFLOWER STEAKS

1 large cauliflower, leaves and stems removed

4 tbsps olive oil, divided

4 tsps smoked paprika

Salt and freshly ground black pepper, to taste

Place the parsley, coriander, mint, spring onion, garlic, lemon juice and olive oil in a food processor or high-speed blender and process until completely smooth. Set aside.

Using a sharp knife, cut the cauliflower into 8 thick slices. Using your hands, rub around a teaspoon of olive oil into each cauliflower piece, then sprinkle with paprika, salt and pepper.

Heat the remaining olive oil (use an extra splash if you need it) in a large frying pan over medium-high heat. Working in batches according to the size of your frying pan, cook the steaks for 4-5 minutes each side until golden brown on the outside and tender, but not crumbly, on the inside.

To serve, place 2 cauliflower steaks on each plate and drizzle with salsa verde.

Roast Cauliflower and Garlic Soup

A RICH, EARTHY AND WARMING SOUP THAT'S IDEAL FOR A COSY
DINNER IN FRONT OF THE FIRE WITH FRIENDS AND FAMILY

SERVES 6

2 heads cauliflower,
broken into florets

1 tbsp olive oil

1 head garlic, cloves
loosened

½ tsp cumin seeds

2 spring onions,
chopped

3 cups (750ml, 24fl oz)
vegetable stock

1 cup (250ml, 8fl oz)
water

1 tsp dried thyme

1 bay leaf

2 cups (500ml, 1pt)
heavy cream

Salt and pepper, to taste

Fresh parsley, chopped,
and pepper to garnish

Preheat the oven to 220°C (430°F, Gas Mark 7) and line a
baking tray with greaseproof paper.

In a large bowl, toss cauliflower pieces with olive oil, garlic,
cumin seeds and spring onions. Spread pieces out onto a
baking tray.

Place in oven and roast for 30 minutes, until golden and tender.
Squeeze the garlic from the cloves and discard the skin.

Transfer cauliflower and garlic mixture to a soup pot and pour in
the vegetable stock and water. Add thyme and bay leaf and bring
to a boil. Reduce to a gentle simmer and cover the pot. Cook for
30 minutes. Remove and discard the bay leaf.

Transfer to a blender and puree in batches, then return to the
pot. Or puree the soup in the pot using an immersion blender,
if you have one.

Stir in the cream and season with salt and pepper. Heat through,
but do not boil, and then serve garnished with chopped parsley
and pepper.

Curry Roasted Cauliflower

SERVES 4

3 garlic cloves, minced

1 medium piece ginger, minced

1 small onion, finely chopped

2 tbsps melted butter or ghee

1 tsp Indian curry powder

Pinch of salt

Ground black pepper

1 small cauliflower, broken into florets

Chopped coriander, to serve

Preheat the oven to 200°C (400°F, Gas Mark 6). Prepare a baking tray lined with greaseproof paper.

Heat a small frying pan over medium-high heat. Add garlic, ginger and onion and fry, stirring, for 10 minutes until sticky and soft.

Mix the melted butter or ghee, curry powder, salt and pepper together in a mixing bowl. Add the cauliflower and garlic-ginger mix and stir to coat.

Transfer to the baking tray arranging in one single layer. Roast for 20 minutes and serve immediately, garnished with chopped coriander.

Creamy Cauliflower Rice

SERVES 4

1 cauliflower head, stem and leaves removed

1 cup (250ml, 8fl oz) coconut milk

1 tbsp minced garlic (optional)

¼ tsp salt

¼ tsp pepper

Roughly chop the cauliflower and feed into a blender gradually, pulsing as you go, until all cauliflower has been added and has formed the consistency of rice.

Add the coconut milk, garlic, if using, salt and pepper and blend on high until well combined.

Transfer to a large frying pan and cook on a medium heat until the cauliflower is hot. Reduce the heat and simmer for 5 minutes. Serve.

CAULIFLOWER

Believe it or not, the cauliflower head is actually an undeveloped flower. And if it were exposed to the sun it would become inedible! Lucky for us it has thick leaves that protect it so we are free to indulge. Cauliflower is a cruciferous vegetable and comes from the same family as broccoli, brussel sprouts, cabbage and kale. Like its cousins, cauliflower is great baked, sauteed, stir-fried and steamed, and adds texture and brightness to any meal. When you're choosing a cauliflower at the store pick one that is firm with creamy white heads and compact florets. Make sure the leaves are a vibrant green colour and look fresh and healthy.

Warm Pumpkin Salad

SERVES 6

800g (1¾ lb) pumpkin, deseeded, skin removed and cut into small wedges

Salt and pepper, to season

1 tbsp fresh marjoram or oregano, chopped

2 tbsps fresh parsley, chopped

4 tbsps olive oil

200g (7oz) rocket

300g (10oz) feta, crumbled

Preheat oven to 220°C (430°F, Gas Mark 7). Line a baking tray with baking paper.

Spread the pumpkin out on the baking tray and sprinkle with salt, pepper, marjoram or oregano and parsley. Drizzle the olive oil over the top and toss to combine. Transfer to the oven to roast for 35 minutes until tender.

To prepare the salad, combine the rocket, feta cheese and pumpkin in a bowl and gently stir to combine.

Beetroot and Orange Salad

SERVES 6

5 medium beetroots, thinly sliced

4 blood oranges

¼ cup (10g, ¼ oz) mint, coarsely chopped

1 tbsp lemon juice

1 tbsp white wine vinegar

1 tsp honey

½ cup (125ml, 4fl oz) olive oil

Salt and freshly ground black pepper

85g (3oz) feta, crumbled

Steam the beetroots for 15 minutes or until tender. Transfer to a bowl and allow to cool completely.

Using a sharp knife, peel the oranges and remove the white pith. Cut into rounds.

Arrange the beetroot and oranges on a serving plate and scatter with feta cheese and mint leaves.

In a small bowl, whisk the lemon juice, vinegar and honey. Whisk in the olive oil and season with salt and pepper. Pour the dressing over the salad.

Duck Breast with Peaches

SWEET, SPICY, TANGY AND CRISPY, THIS DUCK BREAST IS AN EASY AND IMPRESSIVE CHOICE

SERVES 4

4 duck breasts

Salt

Freshly ground black pepper

3 garlic cloves, smashed, but not peeled

3 thyme sprigs

4 ripe peaches, peeled and quartered with pits removed

1 tsp honey

2 tbsps balsamic vinegar

2 tbsps white wine vinegar

2 tbsps port

2 tbsps cold butter, cut into 3 or 4 pieces

Remove the duck breasts from the fridge and bring to room temperature.

Preheat the oven to 250°C (480°F, Gas Mark 9).

Line a baking dish with aluminium foil leaving sufficient overhang to create a tent around the duck.

Lightly score the skin of the duck with a sharp knife, being careful not to cut through to the meat. Rub salt and pepper into the skin.

Heat a large, deep-sided frying pan over a medium-high heat. Place the duck breasts into the pan skin side down and allow to cook for 6-8 minutes until the skin is nicely browned and crispy. Flip and cook on the other side for a further 3 minutes for rare and 5 minutes for medium.

Remove duck from the pan, retaining the pan juices, and transfer to the prepared baking dish. Make a tent with the aluminium foil and crimp the edges before placing in the oven to cook for 5 minutes.

Transfer 1 tablespoon of pan juices into a clean frying pan over a medium heat. Add the garlic and thyme and stir for a minute, then add the peaches. Toss to coat and then lower the heat. Leave the peaches to cook for 5 minutes until soft and golden brown. Remove peaches from the pan and discard the pan fat, retaining any juices.

Still on a low heat, add the honey to the pan and stir for 30 seconds. Then add vinegars and port and bring to a rolling boil. Reduce heat to low and then gradually add the butter, whisking continuously, until a glossy smooth sauce forms. Pour in any leftover juices from the duck and stir to combine. Add duck breasts to the pan and coat with the sauce.

Slice the duck breasts diagonally and serve with the peaches and additional thyme sprigs.

Orange-Glazed Duck

SERVES 6-8

2 x 3kg (7lb) whole ducks

2 tsps salt

½ tsp ground black pepper

1 cup (225g, 8oz) orange marmalade

¼ cup (60ml, 2fl oz) bourbon

3 tbsps honey

1 tbsp fresh lemon juice

¼ tsp ground ginger

Remove the giblets from the ducks, and discard or retain for another use. Rinse ducks, and pat dry with paper towel. Trim the ducks to remove excess fat and skin, then tie legs together with kitchen string. Cover with plastic wrap and transfer to the fridge for up to 24 hours and a minimum of 12 hours.

Preheat oven to 230°C (450°F, Gas Mark 8).

Line a large, deep-sided baking tray with aluminium foil.

Remove ducks from the fridge and bring to room temperature. Prick the legs, thighs and breasts with a fork and then rub well with salt and pepper. Place the ducks on the baking tray, breast side up, and put into the oven to roast for 45 minutes.

While the duck is cooking, make the sauce. Stir together the marmalade, bourbon, honey, lemon juice and ground ginger in a small saucepan over a high heat and bring the mixture to the boil. Reduce heat to medium and cook for a further 10 minutes, stirring frequently, until the sauce has reduced to around 1 cup (250ml, 8fl oz) in volume.

Take the ducks out of the oven and spoon the fat from the pan. Reduce the oven temperature to 180°C (350°F, Gas Mark 4). Using a pastry brush, brush the ducks with the glaze.

Return the ducks to the oven to bake for 20 minutes. Remove and allow to stand for 15 minutes before serving.

Honey-Glazed Confit Duck Leg

SUCCULENT, TENDER, DELICIOUS DUCK THAT'S SURE TO IMPRESS YOUR DINNER PARTY GUESTS AND WARM UP A COLD WINTER'S NIGHT

SERVES 4

4 duck legs

60g (2oz) salt

4 tbsps honey

1 tbsp hoi sin sauce

1 tsp dark soy sauce

1 tbsp black sesame seeds

Salt and ground black pepper, to taste

5 sprigs basil, leaves stripped

Preheat oven to 160°C (325°F, Gas Mark 3).

Transfer duck to an ovenproof baking dish. Sprinkle salt liberally over the duck legs and rub gently into the skin using your hands. Wrap in plastic wrap and set aside to marinate for 30 minutes.

Rinse the salt from the duck and pat dry with a kitchen towel.

Combine 2 tablespoons of the honey, hoi sin, soy and black sesame seeds together in a small bowl. Spread this mixture over the duck and rub it into the skin.

Transfer to the oven and bake for about 1½ hours until meat is very tender. Remove from the oven and set aside to cool. Increase the oven temperature to 200°C (390°F, Gas Mark 6).

Remove the duck legs and place in a roasting pan. Pour over the remaining honey and the basil and return to the oven to roast to crispness for 20 minutes, basting 2-3 times.

Serve with any extra glaze over the top and fresh basil leaves. Serve immediately.

DUCK

A long-standing staple of restaurant menus, particularly Chinese, Thai and French, duck is becoming increasingly popular as a cook-at-home option. But it's a steep learning curve for many of us: where do you buy duck, how do you choose it and how do you cook it?

The buying part is getting easier, as duck breasts, if not the full bird, are commonly available at supermarkets these days. If you live in a rural area, you are likely to have a local butcher with a close connection to the farmer, or you may even be able to buy from the farmer himself at a market stall – then you can quiz him on what to look for and how to cook the thing!

If he's being straight with you, he'll probably say that the duck should have clear, soft skin with no blemishes or tears in it. Beyond that, you have to trust the source.

WHAT TO DO WITH DUCK

Duck meat is naturally moist and very flavoursome, with a fattier texture than other poultry, meaning that cuts such as breasts don't need marinating. Whole ducks are great for roasting, especially if you can master the crispy skin. In European cooking, duck is traditionally paired with fruit – oranges or berries usually – which help to offset the intensity of the flavour and provide a fresh edge to its meatiness. The Asian-style 'Peking' or 'Cantonese duck' is a bit of a process which involves marinating, blanching, hanging and roasting the duck usually over a period of 24 hours or more. It's time well spent, and the results are impressive, but it does require a certain commitment. Luckily there are lots more simple ways to cook duck, such as confit (recipe on page 278) or pan-seared, or using the legs in a casserole.

Duck is a great 'entertaining' food as there is something a little bit special about it, and the pairing with fruity ingredients has a natural decadence to it.

IS IT GOOD FOR YOU?

Duck is a pretty healthy choice. Even though it's fatty, the fat is mostly monounsaturated, which is the same as the 'good fat' found in olive oil. Also, with the skin removed it is lower in fat than chicken. It's also a very good source of protein, zinc and B vitamins.

RED, WHITE OR PINK

Although it's poultry, duck meat is generally considered to be a red meat, unlike chicken which is a white meat. As a red meat, it's common to serve duck a little pink – and it's safe to do so.

Red-Wine Braised Beef Short Ribs

A HEARTY, MEATY DISH THAT WOULD PAIR PERFECTLY WITH A NICE BOTTLE OF CABERNET SAUVIGNON

SERVES 4

3 tbsps butter, divided

8 beef short ribs

Coarse salt

Cracked pepper

2 red onions, chopped

2-3 parsnips, peeled and diced

6 garlic cloves, sliced, reserving some for garnish

2 tbsps chopped fresh rosemary, plus a few sprigs for garnish

750ml (25 fl oz) bottle Zinfandel (or other red wine)

2 cups (500ml, 1pt) beef stock

2 tbsps pink peppercorns

1 tbsp sesame seeds

Preheat oven to 160°C (325°F, Gas Mark 3).

Melt 1 tablespoon of butter in a large Dutch oven or other ovenproof pan.

Sprinkle ribs liberally with coarse salt and pepper. Place the ribs in a single layer in the pan and saute for 10 minutes or until evenly browned on all sides. Remove from the heat and transfer ribs to a large bowl.

Melt 1 tablespoon of butter in the same pan. Add the onions and saute for 5-6 minutes or until golden brown. Next add the parsnips and again saute for 5-6 minutes until golden brown. Stir in the garlic, then the rosemary. Pour the wine and stock into the pan and bring to a boil, using a wooden spoon to scrape any browned bits from the side of the pan.

Return ribs and any juices to the pan, arranging in a single layer. Bring to a simmer and remove from the heat. Decorate with garlic slices and rosemary, and sprinkle the peppercorns and sesame seeds over the top. Cover the dish with a lid or aluminium foil and place in the oven to cook for 2½-3 hours or until very tender.

Note: Can be made up to 2 days ahead. Keep covered in the fridge and re-heat over low heat to serve.

Braised Red Cabbage with Asian Flavours

BRIGHT AND BURSTING WITH FLAVOURS, THIS DISH MAKES FOR A SIMPLE AND ELEGANT ACCOMPANIMENT TO THE MAIN COURSE

SERVES 4-6

1 medium red cabbage

3 apples

Small bunch radishes

1 tsp toasted sesame oil

1 red chilli, finely chopped

3 tbsps white wine vinegar

2-3 tbsps sesame (or nut) oil

1 garlic clove, crushed

Salt and pepper to taste

To prepare the cabbage, rinse it under the tap and discard any old leaves. Pat dry. Quarter the cabbage and remove the core. Place a flat side of the cabbage down on the chopping board and shred using a very sharp knife.

Peel, core and thinly slice the apples.

Wash, trim and thinly slice the radishes.

Heat the sesame oil in a large saucepan over medium-high heat and add the cabbage, apples and radishes. Cook for 4-5 minutes, stirring, until vegetables are soft. Add the chilli, vinegar, oil, garlic, salt and pepper and cook, stirring occasionally, for a further 2-3 minutes, then serve.

Middle Eastern Slow-Cooked Lamb Shanks

WARM FLAVOURS, WAFTS OF ORIENTAL SPICE AND MELTINGLY TENDER MEAT MAKE THIS DISH A WINNER FOR A WINTER'S NIGHT

SERVES 4-6

Olive oil, for frying

6 lamb shanks

12 Asian shallots

8 garlic cloves, crushed

1 tsp ground cumin

1 cinnamon stick

4 star anise

1 orange, zested in strips

2 tbsps tomato paste

3 tbsps pomegranate molasses (or blackstrap molasses)

4 cups (1L, 2pt) chicken stock

Preheat the oven to 160°C (325°F, Gas Mark 3).

Heat the oil in a casserole over a medium heat. Sear the shanks in batches according to the size of your dish for 5 minutes, or until well browned all over.

Remove lamb from the casserole and set aside.

Place the Asian shallots, garlic, cumin, cinnamon, star anise and orange zest into the casserole and stir for 5 minutes or until Asian shallots are just browned. Add tomato paste, pomegranate molasses and stock to the pan and briefly stir to combine the ingredients.

Return the lamb to the casserole over a medium-high heat and bring to the boil. Cover with a lid and transfer to the oven. Cook for 2 hours or more until meat falls away from the bone easily.

Buttery Watercress Mash

A FAVOURITE SIDE DISH THAT'S EASILY TRANSFORMED INTO A CONTEMPORARY AND WONDERFUL ACCOMPANIMENT TO YOUR MEAL

SERVES 4

1.3kg (3lb) Coliban or King Edward potatoes

85g (3oz) butter

3 tbsps milk

2 tbsps creme fraiche

275g (10oz) watercress, stalks removed

2 tbsps lemon juice

Salt and fresh black pepper, to taste

2 tbsps capers (optional)

Wash and peel the potatoes, then cut into even-sized pieces.

Place potatoes in a large saucepan of salted water and bring to the boil. Reduce heat slightly and leave potatoes to cook for at least 20 minutes, and up to half an hour until very tender. Pierce the centre with a fork to test: the centre should be soft. Cook your potatoes well and your mash will be smooth and lump-free, so pay attention to this stage.

Drain the potatoes and return to the pan. Leave for a few minutes to cool slightly and then add butter, milk and creme fraiche.

Using an electric mixer on a slow speed begin to soften and break up the potatoes. Gradually increase the speed as the potatoes become smoother. Add the watercress and beat one last time until light and fluffy.

To finish stir in the lemon juice, salt and pepper and capers, if using.

FANCY MASHED POTATO

Good old mashed potatoes. A dish everyone knows how to cook, right? In one way yes, but in another not. The humble mash has moved on. It's been styled and flavoured and garnered quite a following. And why not, after all, these new-look versions of mashed potato are quite delicious.

MAKING A GOOD MASH

But before we get into that, how about the basic mash: how do you make it creamy, fluffy, light and rich all at the same time? Opinions vary, but here are a few ideas. Most people agree that a starchy potato is a good choice for mash – a potato like Nicolas (creamy) or Coliban (fluffy) usually fit the bill. Cook the potatoes for long enough – if you don't they risk being lumpy. Add cream. Add milk. Don't add cream or milk! Just add butter. Then a bit more butter. Mash with a hand masher, push through a potato ricer, or use a mixer or a blender. As you can see, getting mashed potatoes to your liking is a matter of trial and error, so experiment until you've found your favoured approach.

FANCIFYING YOUR MASH

Mashed potatoes are a fine food on their own and a fine one to fancy up too. The addition of roast garlic makes a beautiful side for a roast dinner. Or you could consider adding a roasted vegetable such as fennel for extra flavour.

Adding cheese – of the Cheddar or cream cheese variety – can make the difference for fussy kids, but adults might appreciate the addition of blue cheese or goat's cheese for mash that's packed full of interesting flavours.

Herb mashed potatoes provide a great opportunity to include your preferred herb in a different element of the dish, rather than on the side or in the sauce. A combination of herbs works well, or you can just choose a favourite with a stronger flavour such as sage or thyme. Don't forget the salt and pepper and perhaps a sprinkle of Parmesan to finish.

It might be taking things too far for some people, but how about mixing up the mash with another root vegetable such as parsnip or pumpkin? This will add flavour and give a different texture to your mash. For a fresh version, try the watercress mash recipe on page 288, or swap the watercress for spinach or artichoke. If you are serving fish, try lemon mashed potatoes.

Don't forget to make fritters from your leftover mashed potato and serve with poached eggs the next morning!

Molten Chocolate Lava Pots

WHO CAN RESIST THESE LITTLE CHOCOLATE VOLCANOES? THEY'RE SURPRISINGLY EASY TO MAKE AND RELIABLY IMPRESSIVE

SERVES 4

215g (8oz) good-quality dark chocolate (60% cacao or more), coarsely chopped

150g (5oz) unsalted butter, cut in large pieces

3 large eggs

3 large egg yolks

¼ cup (55g, 2oz) white sugar

5 tbsps plain flour, sifted

Icing sugar, to finish

Preheat the oven to 160°C (325°F, Gas Mark 3). Butter and flour six individual ovenproof jars.

Bring a pan quarter-filled with water to the boil and reduce to a simmer. Place the chocolate and butter in a heatproof bowl set over the simmering water and allow the chocolate to melt, stirring until smooth. Cool slightly.

Using an electric mixer beat the eggs, yolks and sugar at medium-high speed for 8-10 minutes or until pale and thick. Reduce the speed to low and gradually add the flour.

Scrape the chocolate mixture into the flour mixture, and beat for a further 5 minutes, until thick and glossy.

Divide half of the mixture among the prepared jars. Sprinkle tall but 50g (2oz) of chopped chocolate among them, placing the chunks in the centre of each, then pour over the rest of the batter.

Transfer to the oven to bake for 10-12 minutes, until the cake is set around the edges but the centre wobbles a little when the jar is gently moved from side to side. Set aside to cool for 3-5 minutes before serving.

Serve in the jars, dusted with icing sugar.

Mulled-Wine Poached Pear on Chocolate Mousse

IT DOESN'T HAVE TO BE CHRISTMAS TO ENJOY THESE SPICY POTS OF GOODNESS — BUT IT MIGHT BE!

SERVES 6

POACHED PEARS

750ml (25fl oz) bottle red wine

1½ cups (375ml, 13fl oz) water or orange juice (no pulp)

1 cinnamon stick

3 star anise, whole

10 cloves, whole

1 tsp vanilla essence

2 bay leaves

Juice and zest of 1 orange

Juice and zest of 1 lemon

½ cup (180g, 6 oz) runny honey

½ cup (80g, 3oz) brown sugar

6 ripe pears, peeled and halved

CHOCOLATE MOUSSE

200g (7oz) dark chocolate (70% cacao), broken into pieces

3 cups (750ml, 24fl oz) heavy whipping cream, divided

⅓ cup (50g, 2oz) icing sugar

Chopped nuts, to decorate

In a medium to large saucepan, combine all poached pear ingredients, apart from the pears, and stir together. Place the pears in the saucepan, ensuring that they are fully covered with liquid.

Bring to the boil and then reduce heat to a gentle simmer. Partially cover the pan with a lid and cook in this way for 2 hours, or until pears are tender and a ruby red colour on the exterior. The liquid will have reduced significantly, but be careful to check that it doesn't start to burn.

Every so often during cooking baste the pears with the syrup and once during cooking, turn the pears over to ensure cooking on both sides.

Carefully remove pears and set aside. Boil liquid for 5-10 minutes or until thick and syrupy.

While the pears are cooking, you can make the mousse. First, make the chocolate ganache.

Place the chocolate pieces in a medium bowl. Place ¾ cup (185ml, 6fl oz) cream in a saucepan and bring to a near boil. Pour the cream over the chocolate in the bowl and leave it to stand for 3-4 minutes, then gently stir until fully incorporated and melted. Set aside to cool.

Place the remainder of the cream into the bowl of an electric mixer. Add the icing sugar and mix on medium-low speed until soft peaks start to form. Turn the speed of the mixer down a little and continue to beat until stiff peaks form.

Fold a cup (or thereabouts) of the whipped cream into the chocolate ganache and gently stir to fully incorporate. Repeat this process until all the cream has been incorporated and the mixture is smooth and glossy.

Cover with cling film and transfer to the fridge to chill for a minimum of 1 hour before assembling and serving your dessert.

To serve, place chocolate mousse in individual bowls, topped with two pear halves and garnished with chopped nuts.

Pumpkin Gingersnap Parfait

A GOOEY, CREAMY DESSERT THAT'S PURE INDULGENCE — AND NOT FOR THE FAINT-HEARTED

SERVES 4

90g (3oz) butter

2 cups (250g, 8oz) crushed gingersnap crumbs

2 cups (450g, 1lb) pumpkin puree

½ cup (110g, 4oz) white sugar

⅓ cup (50g, 2oz) brown sugar

¾ cup (185ml, 6fl oz) cream

¾ cup (185ml, 6fl oz) milk

2 eggs

1 tsp vanilla

1 tsp cinnamon

1 tsp ground ginger

½ tsp salt

¼ tsp nutmeg

Pinch of ground cloves

170g (6oz) cream cheese, room temperature

¼ cup (40g, 1½ oz) icing sugar

Pinch of ground ginger

Extra gingersnap biscuits and crumbs, to decorate

CARAMEL SAUCE

1½ cup (235g, 8oz) brown sugar

6 tbsps butter

½ cup (125ml, 4fl oz) cream

1 tsp vanilla essence

Pinch of salt

Preheat oven to 190°C (375°F, Gas Mark 5). Make ready a baking dish.

Melt the butter in a medium saucepan over a medium heat. Add the crushed gingersnaps and stir to fully coat the crumbs in butter.

Press the ginger biscuit mixture into the base of the baking dish using your fingers to ensure it reaches the corners. Transfer to the oven to bake for 5 minutes. Remove from the oven and set aside.

Meanwhile, place the pumpkin, the sugars, cream, milk, eggs, vanilla, cinnamon, ginger, salt, nutmeg and cloves into a large mixing bowl and whisk until well combined.

In a separate mixing bowl, combine the cream cheese, icing sugar and a pinch of ground ginger.

Next, make the simple caramel sauce. Combine all ingredients in a medium saucepan over medium-low heat. Cook, stirring, for 6-7 minutes, until thickened. Reduce heat to very low while you assemble the dessert.

In individual serving glasses, layer gingersnap crumb, cream cheese and pumpkin filling. Finish with caramel sauce and decoration.

Index

HERRON
book distributors

First Published in 2017 by Herron Book Distributors Pty Ltd
14 Manton St
Morningside
QLD 4170
www.herronbooks.com

WWW.CAPTAINHONEY.COM.AU

Custom book production by Captain Honey Pty Ltd
PO Box 155
Byron Bay
NSW 2481
www.captainhoney.com.au

Cataloguing-in-Publication. A catalogue record for this book is available from the National Library of Australia

ISBN 978-0-947163-41-9

Printed and bound in China by Shenzhen Jinhao Color Printing Co., Ltd

5 4 3 2 1   17 18 19 20 21

NOTES FOR THE READER

All reasonable efforts have been made to ensure the accuracy of the content in this book. Information in this book is not intended as a substitute for medical advice. The author and publisher cannot and do not accept any legal duty of care or responsibility in relation to the content in this book, and disclaim any liabilities relating to its use.

PHOTO CREDITS

Front cover: Natasha Breen
Back cover: Anna Moskvina
5 second Studio p 214. 5PH p 52, 229. 13Smile p 217, 215. Africa Studio p 4, 219, 221, 249. Alena Haurylik p 257. Alliance p 263. Alphonsine Sabine p 84. Alvaro German Vilela p 237. Alphonsine Sabine p 83, 97. Anna_Pustynnikova p 173, 212, 214. Anna Hoychuk p 84, 124, 259, 283, 295. Anna Kurzaeva p 45, 145, 210. Andrew Riverside p 43. Alexander Raths p 86. Alisalipa p 16. AS Food studio p 117, 280. Brent Hofacker p 100, 101, 252, 260. Bikeriderlondon p 62. Bogdan Sonjachnyj p 300. Breslavtsev Oleg p 154. Dar1930 p 158. Daxiao Productions p 187. DenisFilm p 125. Ekaterina Glazova p 243. EPSTOCK p 119. from my point of view p 95, 180. Elena Demyanko p 25, 147. Elena Veselova p 1, 13, 31, 33, 61, 88, 109, 155, 190, 201, 251, 262. etorres p 108. Family Business p 149. Foxys Forest Manufacture p 23, 57, 71, 202, 292. Goskova Tatiana p 206. Gourmetphotography p 36. HandmadePictures p182, 226. Hans Geel p 141. hlphoto p 177, 287. Ievgeniia Maslovska p 204. Jan Faukner p 98. Jacob Blount p 170. Jack Frog p 10, 74. Josie Grant p 69. Jmattisson p 38. Joshua Resnick p 175, 228. Julia Tsokur p 240. Kati Molin p 199. Kiian Oksana p 67, 272. kuvona p 195. margouillat photo p 140. Lapina Maria p 124, 272. Larisa Blinova p 76, 161. Iavizzara p 182. LENA GABRILOVICH p 38. Lenakov p 138, 269. Lesya Dolyuk p 53, 133. Liliya Kandrashevich p 105. Lisovskaya Natalia p 64, 156. Llaszlo p 39. Magdanatka p 223, 267. MariaKovaleva p 41, 115, 233, 279. Marija Kerekes p 152. Mariya Siyanko p 135. meringue-pie p 127. merc67 p 107. Michelle Lee Photography p 299. MSPhotographic p 170. Myronovych p 270. Napat Photography p 19. Natasha Breen p 247. Natalia Klenova p 250. Nazarovsergey p183. Nataliya Arzamasova p 185, 189, 268. Neha Aurangabadkar p 24. Odua Images p 81. Oldbunyip p 73. Olena Kaminetska p 167. oneinchpunch p 110, 200. Oxana Denezhkina p 100, 238. Pavel Korotkov p 262. pearl7 p 277. Pilipphoto p 141. Phototasty p 26, 47, 123. Pressmaster p 128. Rawpixel.com p 2, 6.Roboryba p 120.Robyn Mackenzie p 79. sarsmis p 103, 165, 207, 254.SEAGULL_L p 228, 275. Sea Wave p 290. Sebastiana p 168. Shaiith p 24. Shebeko p 50, 151. SimonTheSorcerer p 14. simonidadj p 148. Stephanie Frey p 225. Stockcreations p 21, 60, 90, 206. Stolyevych Yuliya p 29. Stepanek Photography p 12, 34. Steve Cukrov p 171. Svariophoto p 235. svry p 197, 231. ThaiThu p 85. Tukhfatullina Anna p 297. Tanya Stolyarevskaya p 245.Taiftin p 285. Tatiana Volgutova p 93. Tercer Ojo Photography 148. thefoodphotographer p 136, 265, 273. tommaso79 p 178. The Watercress Company p 289. Timeless889 p163. Viennetta p 143. VVDVVD p 209. vm2002 p 268. Wollertz p 164. Yulia-Bogdanova p 55. Yulia Grigoryeva p 48. ziashusha p 53, 165. Zkruger p 59, 192. zi3000 p 90, 91, 112, 131 Images used under license from Shutterstock.com